If you've ever felt overwhelmed [barcode covers text] hasn't?), *All the Feels* will help yo[u] [barcode covers text] joy, and purpose in your emotional life. Elizabeth offers heart-healing hope, delivered in a delightful mix of engaging stories, true confessions, and biblical insights that make you go, "Wow!" Stop letting your emotions get the best of you—and learn how to experience all your emotions in ways that will revolutionize your relationship with yourself, with others, and with God.

**KAREN LINAMEN BOUCHARD**
Author of *Just Hand Over the Chocolate and No One Will Get Hurt* and other inspirational books for women

Elizabeth Laing Thompson has written an interesting, insightful, and easy-to-read book about a very complex subject. The amount of thought and prayer that she has put into this project is obvious. I highly recommend *All the Feels* to anyone who wants to learn how to identify, process, and manage their emotions in a healthy and righteous manner.

**MARY M. SHAPIRO, PHD**
Licensed clinical psychologist

Full of laugh-out-loud stories, practical help, Scripture-based prayers, and powerful reflection prompts, *All the Feels* is one of the best books on emotions I have ever read. An experienced "big feeler" and student of the Bible, Elizabeth Laing Thompson will help you identify the type of feeler you are, the blessing to be found in feelings, and how to keep feelings in their proper place in order to live an untangled and authentic life. So whether you roll out the welcome mat to each and every feeling or try to shove them all in a closet, *All the Feels* is a must read!

**JENNIFER MARSHALL BLEAKLEY**
Author of *Joey* and *Pawverbs*

Dissect any given hour of my day and you'll discover a cornucopia of emotions abounding inside my heart, because *all the things* produce *all the feels* within me. As a result, I often struggle with how to handle my feelings, wondering why God wired me the way he has. But *All the Feels* has helped me untangle the blessedness of all my big emotions by looking at them through the perspective of my bigger God. I no longer believe godliness equates to an emptiness of emotion. I feel because the God who designed me for godliness experiences *all the feels* too. I highly recommend this book for tangled-up hearts everywhere, because Elizabeth Laing Thompson has given us the means to harness our happy and our heartache the way God intended. So enjoy your emotions. Keep feeling all the feels, because our God is doing the same.

**TRACY STEEL**
Speaker and author of *A Redesigned Life: Uncovering God's Purpose When Life Doesn't Go as Planned*

As someone who has thoughts that overwhelm me and emotions that often overtake me, I found *All the Feels* so uplifting to read! Elizabeth just gets it, and because she knows the struggle firsthand, she is able to provide practical tools along with biblical application in order to help someone like me defeat the battle that often rages within. Her stories will have you saying, "Me too." And her insight will have your heart and mind saying, "Thank you."

**ELISHA KEARNS**
Blogger, speaker, and founder of Waiting for Baby Bird Ministries

In a world that often tells us our feelings are "too much" or "not enough," Elizabeth offers a much-needed message infused with encouragement and anchored in God's Word. You'll finish this book equipped to live an emotionally engaged life, secure in the knowledge that the Creator of the universe designed your emotions for a purpose, on purpose.

**HEIDI MCCAHAN**
Inspirational romance author

*All the Feels* is not just for the big feelers. Elizabeth's perspectives are transformative in helping us appreciate a new layer of God's personality through those who feel big. As a steady feeler, I have been woven together by my mom, my son, and my friends who all feel big. *All the Feels* is a practical guide for learning to feel forward and appreciate emotion in ourselves, in others, and in our Father.

**LAURA HOPE WHITAKER**
Speaker and founder of Java Joy and hopesweethome.com

DISCOVER WHY EMOTIONS ARE (MOSTLY) AWESOME AND

# ALL THE FEELS

HOW TO UNTANGLE THEM WHEN THEY'RE NOT

## ELIZABETH
## LAING THOMPSON

TYNDALE
MOMENTUM®

*The Tyndale nonfiction imprint*

Visit Tyndale online at tyndale.com.

Visit Tyndale Momentum online at tyndalemomentum.com.

Visit the author online at ElizabethLaingThompson.com.

TYNDALE, Tyndale's quill logo, Tyndale Momentum, and the Tyndale Momentum logo are registered trademarks of Tyndale House Publishers. Tyndale Momentum is the nonfiction imprint of Tyndale House Publishers, Carol Stream, Illinois.

All the Feels: Discover Why Emotions Are (Mostly) Awesome and How to Untangle Them When They're Not

Designed by Libby Dykstra

Edited by Stephanie Rische

Published in association with the literary agency of Kirkland Media Management, LLC.

For information about special discounts for bulk purchases, please contact Tyndale House Publishers at csresponse@tyndale.com, or call 1-800-323-9400.

**Library of Congress Cataloging-in-Publication Data**
Names: Thompson, Elizabeth Laing, author.
Title: All the feels : discover why emotions are (mostly) awesome and how
    to untangle them when they're not / Elizabeth Laing Thompson.
Description: Carol Stream, Illinois : Tyndale House Publishers, 2020. |
    Includes bibliographical references.
Identifiers: LCCN 2020006461 (print) | LCCN 2020006462 (ebook) |
    ISBN 9781496441799 (trade paperback) | ISBN 9781496441805 (kindle edition) |
    ISBN 9781496441812 (epub) | ISBN 9781496441829 (epub)
Subjects: LCSH: Emotions—Religious aspects—Christianity. | Emotional
    maturity—Religious aspects—Christianity. | Emotions—Biblical teaching.
Classification: LCC BV4597.3 .T46 2020 (print) | LCC BV4597.3 (ebook) |
    DDC 248.4—dc23
LC record available at https://lccn.loc.gov/2020006461
LC ebook record available at https://lccn.loc.gov/2020006462

Printed in the United States of America

| 26 | 25 | 24 | 23 | 22 | 21 | 20 |
|----|----|----|----|----|----|----|
| 7  | 6  | 5  | 4  | 3  | 2  | 1  |

*To Mom and Dad:*

*Thank you for being the safe place for all my feelings all my life:*
*for listening without flinching, shepherding without complaining,*
*and sharing your own emotions without holding back.*
*Thank you for not freaking out (at least not when I was in the*
*room!) when big feelings reached gargantuan proportions.*
*I owe you everything and love you for always.*

# CONTENTS

# PART ONE

# HOW SHOULD WE FEEL ABOUT OUR FEELINGS?

# CHAPTER 1

# WELCOME TO OUR WORLD

I still remember the first time I read the phrase "all the feels." I was scrolling through my Facebook feed, reading comments on a tear-jerker of a poem. A friend had written, "All the feels," with a series of emojis: laughing, crying, laugh-crying. My heart gave a little hiccup, and I laughed to myself. *All the feels? Welcome to my world.*

Maybe, like me, you are a big feeler. A sensitive soul, you live with all the deep feelings all the time. You are captivated by beauty, devastated by loss. The first to love, the last to leave. When you dive deep (and you always dive deep), you may struggle to swim back to the surface. You live in emotional high-definition, noticing—and mourning—the ugly things of life, seeing—and savoring—every gorgeous detail in the beautiful. For as long as you can remember, you've sought to make peace with your powerful feelings, and you long for God to help you sort out your emotional life.

Or maybe you consider yourself a steady feeler: some mood

swings here and there, but most days you stay steady as she goes and avoid major melodrama. But sometimes. Sometimes life grows stormy, faith gets thorny, feelings become unruly—and you need guidance. You wonder how to marry faith and feelings: how to honor God when strong feelings come knocking, how to submit wayward feelings to his ways.

Or maybe you prefer thinking to feeling, and even picking up a book with the word *feel* in the title is already making you twitchy . . . but people keep urging you to "get in touch with your feelings" (go ahead, insert your grunt of protest here), so you're reading even though you're kind of in pain. As a reluctant feeler, you're here to better acquaint yourself with your emotional side—we're talking handshakes, not hugs—and figure out what role feelings should play in your life, especially your spiritual life.

Big feelers, steady feelers, reluctant feelers—we've all got feelings. And no matter how intensely or how often we experience strong feelings, our emotional life is a huge part—a defining part—of our Christian walk. Maybe it has never occurred to us that we can have any say in what we feel, when we feel it, and how long we feel it. Feelings have a mind of their own . . . right? Feelings just do what they do . . . right? Right—that is, unless we learn to take the wheel, giving our emotions some biblical direction and parameters, learning how to feel on purpose.

Figuring out what to do with our emotions—which ones to welcome and how long to let them stay, which ones to limit or avoid, and how in the world to achieve those superhuman feats— is a complex but necessary spiritual skill. One that's essential to finding happiness and hanging onto holiness.

Me? I'm a big feeler—the word *big* being a laughable understatement. If feelings were weight lifters, mine would be a four-hundred-pound guy named Sven, legs the size of tree trunks, who can pull eighteen-wheelers across parking lots with chains clenched

| | WHAT KIND OF FEELER ARE YOU? | Almost always | Sometimes | Rarely |
|---|---|---|---|---|
| 1. | I have difficulty separating facts from feelings. | | | |
| 2. | I am easily overwhelmed. | | | |
| 3. | People tell me I am too sensitive. | | | |
| 4. | I experience mood swings. | | | |
| 5. | I am profoundly moved by beauty or art. | | | |
| 6. | I feel others' pain as if it were my own. | | | |
| 7. | I easily put myself in other people's shoes. | | | |
| 8. | I struggle to shake a mood when it hits. | | | |
| 9. | Gut feelings and instinct play a role in my decision making. | | | |
| 10. | I find it easy to connect with God in worship and prayer. | | | |
| | SUBTOTAL | | | |
| | TOTAL | | | |

**KEY**
Almost always = 3
Sometimes = 2
Rarely = 1

**RESULTS**
22+ = big feeler
15–21 = steady feeler
10–14 = reluctant feeler

in his teeth. Honestly, I used to wish I'd been wired a little less emotionally. Especially when, as a newlywed, I'd get weepy about something—maybe it was hurt feelings or work stress or the ever-skyrocketing price of cereal, who knows?—and my new husband would look at me with a bewildered but affectionate twinkle in his eye and tease, "I never knew I married a sprinkler!" Ha. Ha. *Ha.* (Please read that laughter with an eye roll.)

What was I supposed to do with fear? With anxiety? With the way I hoped so hard I thought my heart might burst from the wanting? With the way I loved people by flinging my whole heart in, leaving myself wide open to soaring joy—and searing hurt?

What was I supposed to do with insecurity and gratitude and sorrow and loss and envy and anger and ambition and the list goes on forever? It took me half a million years to figure out where all my deep feelings fit into my Christian walk. To realize that our faith is exactly the place—the only place!—to process all our feelings.

As a woman who has lived every day of her life having All The Big Feelings All The Day Long, well—I volunteer to be your go-to feelings girl. Whether you have a sensitive soul with more feelings than you know how to name (much less process), a steady flow of emotions somewhere in the middle, or a logic-minded personality occasionally waylaid by feelings you need help interpreting, this book is for you. We've all got emotions. And we all need to learn how to identify, express, experience, and—yes, sometimes wrangle—our feelings.

In the pages to come you'll find scores of Scriptures and practical tips for how to deal with all the feels (even the kind you never asked for). You're feeling sad? Read on to find Scriptures and Bible-based strategies. You're feeling insecure? Keep reading. Angry? Anxious? Disappointed? Hopeful? Grab a cup of coffee and let's settle in for some conversation on relationships, confidence, and where God fits into that messy mix.

Where do all the Scriptures and strategies in this book come from? From a lifetime spent bringing intense emotions to God and learning—sometimes the hard way (translation: the melodramatic and miserable way)—to submit those emotions to him and his Word.

This isn't just a field for psychologists and doctors with lots of initials behind their names. Emotions are everybody's game. And I'm writing this book *because* I'm not a doctor. Not a psychologist, psychiatrist, or any kind of –ist (although I confess that on dark days I can be a pessimist). I'm just a big feeler with a big love for the Bible, a girl who's spent a lifetime seeking to align her emotional life with—and enrich it with—God's will and ways. Along the way, I've assembled a stockpile of Scriptures and a toolbox of emotional practices that have made life in Christ—and life in general—better, deeper, and richer. I can't wait to share them with you. Of course, this book is no replacement for professional help. Sometimes we face emotional situations that require more than the pages of a book can offer. If you find yourself in a circumstance that requires additional support, I pray you seek whatever counsel and care you need.

Before we talk more specifically, step with me into a classic example, borrowed from my college years, of what goes on inside this head and heart of mine. Perhaps you'll relate (though for your sake, I hope you relate to a less dramatic degree).

## ONCE UPON A TIME, IN THE LIFE OF A BIG FEELER

The student worship night has ended. While all the other college students hang out and have fun in the sanctuary, I've retreated to one of the Sunday school classrooms, the one with the pastel Noah's ark border, trying to catch up on schoolwork. Sitting cross-legged on the carpeted floor, I am a stressed-out island surrounded by a sea of school supplies: battered green backpack, barely-read copy of *The Odyssey*, Greek dictionary, notebooks, flash cards, pens, highlighters. *Behind, behind, I'm so behind.*

Guilt and shame swirl inside, an eddy with tornado potential. *How did I let this happen?* If I'd been reading a little every day like my professors told me to, I wouldn't be eight hundred pages behind and spending precious weekend hours cramming. Fear enters the mix as my old nemesis, Worst-Case Scenario Disorder, rears its ridiculous head: *What if I fail Greek Civ? I've never failed a class in my life, but there's a first time for everything, and if I fail I'm totally wasting Mom and Dad's money, and then they'll pull me out of school and I'll fall apart and lose all hope and ambition and end up scooping ice cream for the rest of my life and—*

"Knock, knock." My thoughts blink off, momentarily stunned, a squirrel in the street.

The Boy is standing just inside the door. Leaning against the doorframe all casual and *I-know-I'm-cute-so-sue-me*.

My heart does a cartwheel.

Fighting the dopey grin that wants to hijack my mouth whenever he's around, I spare him a tight-lipped, *no-I-don't-think-you're-the-most-beautiful-human-alive smile*, and brace myself: Here's the part where he flashes me a stiff grin and then rushes off to find the person he was actually looking for.

"Hi," he says, flashing me a totally not-stiff grin.

"Hi?" I say, then force my eyeballs not to roll. *Why'd you have to tack a question mark onto that "hi," Elizabeth? Just say hi! Exclamation point!*

Then: *Did he come in here on purpose? Was he looking for me?*

The eddy of feelings reverses direction, a different kind of stress: a swirl of lovesick longing.

*Easy with the hoping. He's probably looking for someone else. He's always looking for someone else.*

I dig into my bag and shove a piece of gum into my mouth, my only resistance against the flood of inane comments trying to bubble up my throat. *Don't babble, just chew. Ignore him and go back to your books and your angst.*

But then The Boy plops down beside me, folding his mile-long legs up and hugging them to his chest. Settling in for a chat.

We're sitting alone in a room.

Just the two of us.

I half-choke on my gum, making a horrifying gargly noise, which I try to cover with a cough.

"So . . . whatcha doin'?" he says, and his Georgia drawl does something squirmy to my stomach.

"Oh, you know, berating myself for procrastinating in between pondering the influence of Greek culture on biblical writers. The usual." I give what I know is a borderline flirtatious grin, then barely suppress an I-hate-myself groan. *Could you have possibly given a more dorky response, Elizabeth? Now he thinks you're a vocabulary show-off and a Bible nerd. On top of being a school nerd. So basically, you're a triple nerd. Not to mention a very bad flirt—and isn't flirting a sin?* Guilt-tinged worry prods at my conscience.

I duck my head and start shoving my stuff rather violently into my bag. *Must shut this conversation down before more humiliations pile up.* I wait for The Boy to get bored and leave, but he stretches out his legs and leans back on his elbows, like he plans to stay awhile. Confused, I slow down my packing.

He flicks a finger at my imitation Doc Martens. "New boots?"

My cheeks, foul traitors, blaze with pleasure. *He noticed!* "Yep," I say, trying to affect a casual shrug. "They're really comfortable. And they were on sale, so . . . yeah." *Babbling. UGH.*

My eyes dart up to meet his. Usually this is when we both look away—he because he's waving hello to another football player or sporty girl, me because I'm trying not to let him see me swoon—but tonight he holds my gaze, and I dare to hold his back. His eyes are brown, coffee brown—no, chocolate brown. No, coffee *with* chocolate brown. No matter, I adore both. It must be a sign.

"I like them," he says, sliding me one of his side-smiles.

"Thanks." I drop my eyes back to my boots, hoping he doesn't realize my heart has sprouted wings.

He stretches, yawns. "Well, I guess it's time to head back to campus."

"Yeah," I say. "About that time. Can I still get a ride?"

He smacks my shoulder. "Always." He winks.

My heart bursts out of my chest and zings around the room in a hallelujah dance. *He said "always"! Like a little promise. We're totally getting married.*

I shake my head, trying to calm my chaotic thoughts, crush my idiotic hopes. *Don't be a fool, Elizabeth.* I stumble to my feet, fumble my backpack onto my shoulder, and traipse behind him, new boots squeaking, already planning how I'm going to call my best friend, Sara, and spend four hours breaking down every nuance of this four-minute conversation. After that I can get back to my regularly scheduled guilt trip.

Welcome to life with all the feels, all the time.

It took me many years in Christ to get comfortable with the emotional sides of my character—wait, who am I kidding? I don't have a side that *isn't* emotional. It took me ages to realize that as Christians, we can lead our feelings instead of having our feelings always lead us. It took me forever to understand that emotions can be a defining part of who we are, but that each day's emotions don't have to define that day. And what a revelation it was when I realized that my emotional nature—and yours, too, whether you have all the feels, some of the feels, or reluctant feels—is from God.

## FEELING IN HIS IMAGE

Feelings and all, God the great Artist made us exactly as he wants us to be. His loving hands knit us together in our mother's womb (see Psalm 139:13)—and our emotional capacity is a precious gift. Made in the image of God, we reflect his nature not just physically, but emotionally. And what a passionate God he is! We feel because *he* feels. We love wildly and give lavishly because *he* shows us how.

In this passage we find a small sample of the multihued emotional palette from which our God paints:

I will tell of the kindnesses of the LORD . . .
   yes, the many good things he has done
     for the house of Israel,

according to his compassion and many kindnesses.
He said, "Surely they are my people,
    sons who will not be false to me";
    and so he became their Savior.
In all their distress he too was distressed,
    and the angel of his presence saved them.
In his love and mercy he redeemed them;
    he lifted them up and carried them
    all the days of old.
Yet they rebelled
    and grieved his Holy Spirit.

ISAIAH 63:7-10

In these few lines we glimpse God's compassion, kindness, devotion, affection, protectiveness, empathy, generosity, distress, mercy, hurt, and grief. If we are sometimes sensitive, our God is infinitely more so. He delights, he dotes, he protects. He mourns, he grieves, he shouts with joy. The universe with all its beauty and danger—sunsets and tsunamis, wildfires and fireflies—reflects the many facets and feelings of our mighty, passionate God. The very skies proclaim his artistry, his lyricism, his love of the poetic and ineffable. Every morning his sunrise sings hallelujah; each night his sunset cries, "Glory."

We should not be surprised, then, when we are like him, having powerful feelings—some of us some of the time, some of us all of the time. One of my favorite Bible scenes unfolds in Ezra 3. Whenever I read it, I stand riveted—and affirmed. I think, *Here are my people: deep-feeling, wild-dreaming. And here is our God: all-loving, heart-healing.* Years earlier, faithful Israel had been banished into the humiliation of exile. Long years they had languished, homeless and heartsick, their pain compounded by regret and shame, knowing their suffering was a consequence of their own disobedience. Home was now little more than a memory: Jerusalem, with its festivals, its lavish Temple, its rich history, was gone—all gone. Destroyed. Out of reach.

But finally—finally!—God opened a way for their return, and with slow hands and cautious hearts, they began to rebuild their lives, their nation, their faith. For months the entire community labored together to rebuild the Temple, a home for the God they had once abandoned but were now determined to serve anew. When the foundation of the Temple was complete—the work far from over, but still beautifully begun—they paused the work to celebrate, commemorate:

> When the builders laid the foundation of the temple
> of the LORD, the priests in their vestments and with
> trumpets, and the Levites (the sons of Asaph) with
> cymbals, took their places to praise the LORD, as
> prescribed by David king of Israel. With praise and
> thanksgiving they sang to the LORD:
>
> "He is good;
>     his love toward Israel endures forever."
>
> And all the people gave a great shout of praise to
> the LORD, because the foundation of the house of
> the LORD was laid. But many of the older priests and
> Levites and family heads, who had seen the former
> temple, wept aloud when they saw the foundation of this
> temple being laid, while many others shouted for joy. No
> one could distinguish the sound of the shouts of joy from
> the sound of weeping, because the people made so much
> noise. And the sound was heard far away.
>
> EZRA 3:10-13

Can't you see it, hear it, feel it? The sea of people with streaming eyes and shouting mouths, raised arms and bent knees? The cry so loud the distant people could hear? Laughter and wails, cries of sorrow and shouts of triumph all amingle in one cacophonous roar, a howl so earth shaking and heart wrenching it rumbled down into the earth and surged back up through the soles of their feet—up, up—till it set their souls to trembling?

The children of God: home at last, forgiven at last. The lost Temple: rising from ruin, resurrecting hope. The old ones, the ones who remembered the glory of Solomon's Temple—now they looked on with throats clogged and eyes clouded with memories: far-off, sacred, untouchable. And the young ones, the ones who had lived an estranged half-life in a foreign land, knowing their true home only in stories and borrowed memories—now they cast eyes upon and took first steps into a new life, a free future . . . all they had hardly dared to hope and never hoped to touch. Regret and renewal, longing and loss—where does one feeling end and another begin?

Oh, God's people are emotional people, because they love—and are loved by—an emotional God.

If you have always kept your faith in one compartment of your heart and your emotional life in another, get ready for something new. Get ready to bring God to your emotions and your emotions to God—the God who invented feelings and who now welcomes yours.

## BEHIND THE DOOR OF YOUR HEART

In the pages ahead, I invite you to throw open the doors of your heart as we explore what God has to say about feelings. And you might be surprised to discover how much God has to say about feelings!

If you feel bored with faith, stiff or distant when you pray; if you secretly feel that your faith doesn't apply to your "real life," perhaps you have never learned how to bring your true feelings to God. Perhaps you never knew you could: *God's got the universe to run. Why would he care that I'm having a bad day? That I'm lonely or anxious? That I'm so happy I'm about to dance with a lamppost and sing in the rain?*

Maybe on Sunday mornings you put your feelings in airplane mode (*I'll deal with you after church*), walk into church all shiny and presentable, and wonder why you don't *feel* anything in worship. Why God feels distant and intimidating, or perhaps vaguely disapproving, like a relative you admire from afar. But then you hear other Christians talk about being "close to God," and you're stumped. *"Close to God?" What does that even mean?* It sounds weird . . . but wonderful. When service ends, you walk back out to your car, hoist your emotional burdens back onto your weary shoulders, and wonder what you're missing.

Deep down, we all long for more with God, more from faith. And we all need help with our feelings. In the pages to come, you'll find that God cares deeply about your feelings. If it matters to you, it matters to him. He longs to share your joys, guide your heart, and—most wondrous of gifts—carry your sorrows.

Whether you consider yourself a big feeler, a steady feeler, or a reluctant feeler, in the pages to come you'll find God-centered guidance for your specific emotional needs. First we'll do a drone-style flyover, mapping out the big-picture view. How does God want us to feel about our feelings? What foundational, biblical truths do we need to embrace in order to construct an emotional life that is healthy, happy, and holy? What biblical principles need to undergird our emotional life, giving it stability? And then there are more practical matters: How do we distinguish fact from feeling, and should we trust our feelings? Do we get any choice in which emotions we experience and how intensely we feel them? Which emotional gifts does God want us to expand, explore, and offer to his service?

From there we'll take a closer look at specific feelings and emotional tendencies that can give us trouble: anxiety, sadness, cynicism, idealism, burden-borrowing, guilt, and more. What does the Bible have to say about these feelings, and what practical tools can we add to our emotional toolbox?

In the final section, we'll consider how our emotions affect our spiritual life, and we'll draw out the spiritual skills every Christian must develop in order to cultivate a healthy emotional-spiritual life. How do our feelings flare up when we read difficult passages in Scripture, and what do we do about that? What emotional pitfalls can we avoid in our relationships, and what strengths can we nurture? What effect does social media have on our emotional-spiritual life? We'll come full circle by envisioning how we can use our emotional makeup and gifts to draw closer to God than we've ever been, and how we might devote our particular temperament to his glory.

*   *   *

In the pages to come, I pray you will find more happy and learn how to stay holy. I pray you will be inspired by the wondrous possibilities your emotional nature allows. Emboldened to embrace the beautiful soul God dreamed you would be. Equipped with more of the biblical perspectives, practical tools, and scriptural arsenal you need to encourage your faith, protect your joy, and amplify your strengths.

Like me, perhaps you feel excited about the journey to come. Intimidated by the need to grow. Giddy about spiritual discovery. Nervous about diving deeper. Humbled, eager, overwhelmed, inadequate, understood, comforted, valued . . . well, you know. All the feels.

## FEELING YOUR WAY FORWARD

At the end of every chapter, you'll find material to help you apply what you've read to your walk with God. The prayer prompts are emotionally rich prayers drawn from Scripture, particularly the Psalms. You can borrow the psalmists' exact words and speak them to God, or you can use them as springboards for prayers of your own. The journal prompts are questions for self-reflection that will help you think about how the principles and practices in this book might apply to your daily life. Even if you don't usually journal, I recommend writing down your answers. The act of moving pen across paper cements truth more deeply into our hearts and memories, and it gives us a record of our thoughts and growth over time.

### Prayer Prompt

You are my God; have mercy on me, Lord,
 for I call to you all day long.
Bring joy to your servant, Lord,
 for I put my trust in you.

You, Lord, are forgiving and good,
 abounding in love to all who call to you.
Hear my prayer, LORD;
 listen to my cry for mercy.
When I am in distress, I call to you,
 because you answer me.

PSALM 86:2-7

## Journal Prompts

1. What do you most love about your emotional side? What do you think God most loves about you?

2. What strengths does your emotional disposition give you? How might you use those gifts to honor God and love people?

3. If you could change one trait about your emotional makeup, what would it be? Why?

# CHAPTER 2

# EMBRACING YOUR EMOTIONAL GIFTS

I'm sitting in my quiet-time spot—the comfy chair in the corner between two windows. I'm reading, praying, waiting.

The earth is hushed but alert, night's velvet black giving way to barely there gray. The air holds a stillness, a reverence, as if the world—sky, stars, animals, sleeping humans under covers—holds its breath, awaiting his call, awaiting the sun.

I am praying my way through Psalm 139 for the thousandth time: "You have searched me, LORD, and you know me. You know when I sit and when I rise; you perceive my thoughts from afar. You discern my going out and my lying down; you are familiar with all my ways. Before a word is on my tongue you, LORD, know it completely. You hem me in behind and before, and you lay your hand upon me. Such knowledge is too wonderful for me . . ."

*Oh, God, thank you that you are bighearted, passionate, and affec-tionate—that you feel all the feelings I do—just without any of the sin. It makes me realize that I'm . . . I'm a little bit like you. I mean, not perfect, but—I feel kind of the way you feel.*

I read on: "For you created my inmost being; you knit me together in my mother's womb. I praise you because I am"—my breath catches—"fearfully and wonderfully made." I've read these words before—a thousand times I've read them—but now I stop. I meditate.

*My inmost being.* The real me. The inner me. Complex, bewildering, highly strung, deeply moved, easily weeping, fiercely loving me.

Outside, the gray takes hold. A lone bird sings one tentative note; the other birds' silence rebukes the intrusion. *Too soon.* Fog creeps across the ground, tickling the grass. *Wake up. The sun is coming.*

Fearfully made.

Wonderfully made.

Fearful.

Wonderful.

Wonder-full.

Long minutes I sit and ponder. Even though I've always felt free to express all my deep feelings at home and with God, I have always secretly—almost unconsciously—felt like my intensity was a weakness, particularly when it came to my faith. I have always been *too* everything: too intense, too excitable, too trusting, too "all in," too hopeful, too devastated by disappointment, too heartbroken by pain. Surely all of this must be frailty, a sign of immature faith. Surely all these feelings were detriments to clear thinking and faithful living. Surely all my emotions were distractions from the Christian I imagined I should be: steadfast, unflappable, tough; striding through conflict and crisis with my head high, my path clear, my relationships unclouded by sentiment.

Truth dawns: soul-affirming, axis-shifting, dizzy-making truth.

Laugh-crying, I stutter a prayer. *You made me this way! Your hands shaped this emotional soul of mine. And you* like *me this way!* I clap my hands over my mouth to hold in a cry. If I wake the house, this alone-with-God moment ends. *It wasn't a mistake.* I'm *not a mistake! All this passion, all these feelings—they're not flaw or weakness or sin. You made me this way, and it makes you happy when I'm me. When I'm awestruck by clouds and weak-kneed by music and dreaming wild and loving so hard I think my heart will split in half. Because in all this, I reflect you. I honor you. In all this, I am like you.*

I sit tear-blinking, thunderstruck. In all my years of following God, it has never occurred to me that my emotional nature might be a gift from God. Might be *strength*, not weakness. Might make him happy. Might honor him. And might even *reflect* him in this world—show people little bits of him.

*   *   *

I pray that you, too, will awake as I did that joy-tipped morning. Awake to the pieces of himself that God put in you—divine sparks he lit so you would shine as he does:

> Wake up, sleeper,
>> rise from the dead,
>> and Christ will shine on you.
>
> EPHESIANS 5:14

Oh, how beautiful you are! How gifted by God! How loved and admired and carefully crafted and delighted in and sung over you are!

Now . . . what to do with all that fearful wonderfulness inside you? What purpose does it serve? Because God does not waste gifts. He does not hand them out haphazardly, for no reason. God entrusts us with our emotions, our sensitivities, and it is our job to figure out how best to use those gifts.

## TAKING OFF THE BLINDERS

First things first. What *are* our gifts? How do the different types of feelers reflect the heart of God in this world? Before we dive in, let's acknowledge a difficulty that seems to especially plague those of us who fall on the more sensitive side of the feelings spectrum: we may struggle when it comes to self-analysis. We can readily see where others are gifted, how others should serve, where others are best utilized and fulfilled. But when it comes to assessing ourselves? Deep feelers can be self-blind. We may view our sensitivity as a hindrance, a weakness, a problem to wrestle into submission. In our own view, our weaknesses loom large and hideous; our strengths shrink ever smaller. Even our gifts seem to have less oomph, less punch, less pizzazz. Why? Because many of our greatest gifts are inner strengths, invisible to the wide world.

No one can see us sitting there offering all that beautiful empathy, instinctively understanding what someone else feels and needs. No one can hear us thinking all these insightful thoughts. No one can see the joy flooding through us as we walk along the sidewalk, awed by a cloud-smeared sky. All they see is a space cadet who won't look where she's going and keeps tripping over bumps in the sidewalk.

Many of the sensitive soul's most valuable gifts—compassion, insight, instinct, a knack for listening—won't chart so well on a résumé. And yet these are some of the most impressive assets we have to offer to a school, a church, a family, a team, a workplace. Invaluable as these traits are, they are quiet. Unobtrusive. Subtle.

We're going to take off the blinders and look for all the feeling types' gifts—including our own—and I implore you, please don't run away from this part of the conversation. Don't try to deflect attention to someone else. It's just you and this book, and it's okay to look inward for a few moments. It's okay—indeed, it's right—to give God glory by recognizing and then using the gifts he has invested in you. So what unique contributions do the different types of feelers bring to the world, and where do you fit in?

## What Reluctant Feelers Have to Offer

1. Reluctant feelers help people through hardship.

    They are safe harbors in storms. Providers and protectors.

    When life knocks a person down and the world crumbles beneath their feet, they want to lean on someone who is unchanging and reliable, trustworthy and true. The reluctant feeler's gifts of logic and constancy make them a dependable source of safety, protection, and wisdom.

2. Reluctant feelers help to preserve justice.

    They are fair-minded listeners, defenders of truth.

    Not easily ensnared by gossip, petty conflict, or prejudice, reluctant feelers can rise above arguments to discern truth. Because they are not easily enamored by selfish ambition or swayed by others' opinions, they aren't afraid to speak up for what's right.

3. Reluctant feelers help people solve problems.

    They are fact sifters, solution finders, crisis managers.

    Because reluctant feelers are able to take a step back from emotionally charged situations, they can see past the feelings and drama that may distract more emotional people and say, "Yes, everyone has a lot of feelings about this. But what needs to be *done*?" When crises come, the reluctant feeler's ability to "box up" emotions for a time means they can isolate emotions from solutions and make decisions—even hard ones.

4. Reluctant feelers help more emotional people preserve their relationships.

They are peacemakers, guides, leaders.

The reluctant feeler's commitment to fairness makes their analysis trustworthy. Their integrity makes their counsel unprejudiced. Their levelheadedness makes their advice dependable. All this makes the reluctant feeler an invaluable guide when relationships need protecting, mending, and directing.

## What Steady Feelers Have to Offer

1. Steady feelers help other people manage their feelings.

They are shoulders to cry on, compassionate confidants.

The steady feeler is unique in that they experience strong emotion but rarely get swept away by it. This allows them to relate to and comfort people who are experiencing intense emotions but also to fly above the fray, remaining steadfast and strong. As emotionally intelligent listeners, steady feelers empathize without making things too personal.

2. Steady feelers are able to multitask emotionally.

They are many-hat-wearing adapters.

Because the steady feeler is able to experience and intake a range of emotions without getting easily overwhelmed, they can meet multiple needs. They can wear many relational hats—friend, listener, comforter, counselor, solution finder, and more—and can change roles with ease. When it's inappropriate to spiral out emotionally, steady feelers find a way to muscle through and remain a source of strength for others. They possess the skill of placing their emotions in a holding pattern until the right time. Their resilience means that even when they feel strongly, they can still function effectively.

3. Steady feelers help people feel understood while actively meeting their needs.

They are compassionate and capable caretakers.

Because they experience a broad range of emotions, steady feelers are able to feel with and for hurting people while still maintaining forward motion, thinking and planning and providing for needs.

4. Steady feelers motivate people.

They are inspiring and forward moving.

The steady feeler's ongoing personal experience with emotion allows them to connect with others. This connection means they can inspire and motivate others on a heart level even as they think, plan, and act. These gifts make many steady feelers well suited for leadership roles.

## What Big Feelers Have to Offer

1. Big feelers help people notice.

They are eyes and ears. Receptors and recorders.

They don't just see; they notice. Details do not escape their eyes; small things do not escape their hearts. Their gifts of observation mean they may find the wonder in the ordinary or discern the problem in a plan.

They see other people as they truly are—a natural result of the way they listen and empathize carefully. They see people, they hear people, they understand and celebrate and value (and occasionally revile) people for who they really are. They may notice the quiet person others overlook or appreciate the contributions of people in the background.

2. Big feelers help people understand.

They are translators.

Their empathy and insight allow them to help people who are less observant or emotional to consider the perspective of others who baffle them. What a gift they can be to a minister, a boss, a coworker, a friend, or a parent who has a child they don't understand!

3. Big feelers help people appreciate.

They are encouragers.

They have a colossal capacity for appreciation. If they choose to make themselves vulnerable and lavish the full magnitude of their gratitude on others, they are capable of offering unparalleled joy and encouragement. Their words can make someone's *life*. (Side note: If you are a big feeler, you may need to learn, as I have, to express admiration and gratitude without expecting it in return. Unless the other person is also a big feeler, they rarely know how to respond in kind—and that's okay. They have their gifts; we have ours.)

4. Big feelers help people celebrate.

They are tasters, savorers, connoisseurs of joy.

In my family, my husband drives us forward, keeps us moving. I slow us down. I am the one who makes memories out of moments, who stops in the middle of a chaotic dinner to whisper, "Kevin, this is what we prayed for all those long infertile years. *This.* This madness, this giggling, this talking-over-the-top-of-each-other. Isn't God so good, and isn't it even better than we thought?"

5. Big feelers model vulnerability.

They are soul sharers.

Big feelers have the capacity for deep emotional expression. This is a role—both beautiful and terrifying—they can play in this world. But so many of us sensitive types shrink from it. We have been told that emotion is weakness, so we stuff it. We keep it to ourselves. We don't like being vulnerable—it makes us feel . . . well, vulnerable! Some of us don't enjoy the fact that our emotions are permanently connected to our tear ducts. But if we don't model vulnerability—we who so readily, so fully, feel all the feels—how will the more reluctant or even stoic people of the world ever learn to find their feelings?

6. Big feelers feel—and demonstrate—love.

They are givers.

They love hard and long. And I'm talking about all types of loves, not just romantic love. (But oh, how we *could* talk about romance—we are the ones who get *Romeo and Juliet*—the falling hard, the ecstatic high, the melodramatic sense that life is not worth living if a relationship ends.)

When big feelers love, they go all in. Some rush in full steam ahead from the get-go, easily caught up in a surge of feeling; others have learned caution the hard way, so they wait and guard their hearts until they just can't hold back any longer and they *have* to love with the full force of their feelings.

As a big feeler, you may be the first—maybe even the only—person on earth who is emotionally capable of giving another person a taste of what it means to be loved by God in heaven. They may not believe God loves them until they know you do. By showing love—big, brave love—we reflect God's heart for his children.

7. Big feelers offer insight.

They are sages.

Pair acute observation with deep thinking, and you've got the gift of insight. Wisdom. The gift of *interpreting* what we see.

Insight is a gift we have to develop the confidence to use. Big feelers tend to hold back on offering their insights, partly out of respect for others' feelings, out of reluctance to overstep boundaries. They are hesitant to interrupt, to speak up too loudly, to take up too much space or attention in a conversation or meeting. If other people have things to say, we sensitive types feel emotionally bound to hear and appreciate and validate those things . . . so we may stifle our thoughts out of respect for others'. (This is not to suggest that all sensitive souls are quiet or introverted. Many an extrovert is also a big feeler.)

Even if big feelers are confident in speaking up, they sometimes have a difficult time expressing a confident opinion or taking a side, because they see both sides of an issue. They often see multiple additional sides of an argument that the rest of the group hasn't even thought of yet. And so they reserve judgment, withhold comment.

Insight is a gift I hope you'll take the time to cultivate, to pray about, and to use. If you feel stuck, seek counsel from family, friends, or coworkers on how you can offer your insights at home, at church, at work.

## WIRED FOR CONNECTION

Want to know one more amazing thing about all these dazzling gifts? You can share your talents, even without an official role. You don't need to be appointed The Grand Official Listener, Sympathy Show-er, or Wisdom Giver in order to listen, show sympathy, or give wisdom. You don't need to be anointed The Steadfast Shoulder to Cry On, Rock to Lean On, or Quick Thinker in a Crisis in order to share your strength, dependability, or competence. And you can use your gifts everywhere—at home, at school, at work, at church, on the bus, in a dorm, in lines and online—you can serve anywhere and anyone.

So what does it look like when we employ our gifts? How do they serve us in daily life, in real relationships? Here's an example from my own marriage. (You will read many stories in this book about the ways my preacher husband, Kevin, helps me navigate my sensitivities, but sometimes my sensitivities help him too.)

\* \* \*

Kevin bangs through the front door and drops his bag to the floor with more force than necessary. It's been many years since he complimented my boots that fateful Friday night, but my heart still does a little jig when he enters the room. Four shrieking comets— our offspring—hurtle into his knees. Above their heads, I see him attempt his usual cheery greeting, but his voice is distracted, strained.

Kevin, a classic steady feeler—empathetic, but also fair minded and even keeled—hardly ever sounds upset. My heart takes a nervous dip. "What's wrong?"

He holds up a finger, grabs a squealing kid under each arm, and lumbers toward the couch in the playroom with the other two clinging to his ankles. One by one, he tosses them into the "trash" (aka the couch). They scream with glee, clamoring for more. "I need to talk to Mommy," he says, shutting the playroom door on their disappointed moans.

"I don't get it," he says, raking a hand through his black hair, making it spike up and out—think Charlie Sheen, circa 1986. "I met with Jack, and he said he feels like I don't listen to him. I think that's the third person who's told me that this month. I listen, don't I? You feel like I listen, right?"

I blink, sorting thoughts. "Well, I—"

"*All I do* is listen to people! And I bite my tongue *all the time*." He grabs a Bible off the coffee table and waves it around. "Do you know how many things I want to say but don't?"

"Well—"

Kevin starts pacing. "And I'm patient! So patient! And pleasant! I'm pleasant, right? You always say I'm pleasant." He points the Bible at me like a sword.

I offer a squinty half-smile, trying to soften my words: "Do you want me to respond, or do you just want me to listen while you vent about what a good listener you are?"

Kevin opens his mouth, raises a finger, then smacks himself in the face. He gives a sheepish almost-smile before mumbling, "I want to listen." He sinks onto the couch, hands and Bible between his knees.

"You know I think you are the best person on the planet, and yes, you are wonderfully pleasant when you are not endangering people with your violent Bible-brandishing." This pulls a half-laugh out of him. "But I do think there are some times you don't realize how you come across. And"—I step forward to squeeze his arm so he knows I'm not trying to be mean—"it might take me a minute to get this out, so it would be great if you'd let me talk till I'm done. Okay?"

Kevin gives a rather begrudging nod.

"Mmm-kay, so . . . you know how in the middle school locker room all those guys ganged up on you and jumped you for no reason? And you just closed your eyes and started swinging? You figured that if you punched back hard and fast, they wouldn't try messing with you again?"

"Well, it worked, didn't it?" He shrugs, flashing a smug half-smile.

"I know, but . . . I think you're still doing it. When you feel criticized, your instinctive response is to punch back, hard and fast. I've learned that you always calm down after a minute or two, and if I just give you a little time to breathe, we work things out quickly. But other people don't know you as well as I do. So when they say something you don't like and you get defensive and punch back, they just back off and shut down."

"But I—"

I tap his arm again. "And that's the second thing. You start talking before people are done. You're good at expressing your thoughts quickly, but most people aren't. You start responding when they've barely gotten started talking."

I wait, expecting a reaction, but Kevin just nods. I keep going. "The thing is, it takes people even *longer* to get their feelings out when they're talking to you, because—well, as a preacher, you're an authority figure, which makes you intimidating; plus you're tall and handsome"—I give him what I hope is an encouraging wink—"which makes you doubly intimidating."

He rolls his eyes but smiles.

I plow ahead. "I think you have to train yourself to stop punching back. To *thank* people for bringing up whatever it is that's bothering them—even if you disagree—and then invite them to get it all out. You might want to make it a habit to say, 'And what else?' And then let them talk more. And then say, 'And what else?' And let them talk even more. Lather, rinse, repeat, as many times as necessary."

Kevin heaves a sigh and chokes out, "Thank you. And what else?"

*   *   *

One of my roles as the big feeler in our marriage is to help steady Kevin grow in his sensitivity. To help him see hard things that his ever-so-optimistic perspective sometimes overlooks. He doesn't mean to throw a happy filter over everything, but sometimes he does. He doesn't intentionally cut people short while they are still putting words together, but sometimes he does. He doesn't mean to miss their cues, but sometimes he does.

Just as I need his logic, positivity, and relentless joy (as you will see in many stories in this book), he also needs my insight, observations, and awareness of nuance. He needs my honesty. Yes, he is a gifted minister, but he needs me to help him not just minister *to* people—meet needs, make plans, preach sermons—but connect *with* people. To see them. Hear them. Understand them.

## FANNING YOUR GIFTS INTO FLAME

Listen to Peter's words about using our gifts for God and his people:

> Each of you should use whatever gift you have received
> to serve others, as faithful stewards of God's grace in its
> various forms. If anyone speaks, they should do so as one
> who speaks the very words of God. If anyone serves, they
> should do so with the strength God provides, so that in
> all things God may be praised through Jesus Christ. To
> him be the glory and the power for ever and ever. Amen.
> 1 PETER 4:10-11

Your emotional and intuitive giftedness are God's grace to you—and through you, they are God's grace to other people.

I encourage you to "fan into flame" whatever gifts God has given you—to use those gifts to the fullest capacity (2 Timothy 1:6). If you show compassion, do it with the bigheartedness God has given you. If you have insights to offer from your observations and keen sense about people, offer those insights with humble confidence. If your tenderness drives you to serve, then serve with the strength God provides.

Are you ready to give? Ready to shine? In the chapters ahead, we will talk about how we can use our God-given emotions most effectively in different areas of our lives. Let's start in the most emotional place of all: at home.

## FEELING YOUR WAY FORWARD

### Prayer Prompt

You created my inmost being;
    you knit me together in my mother's womb.
I praise you because I am fearfully and wonderfully made;
    your works are wonderful,
    I know that full well.
My frame was not hidden from you
    when I was made in the secret place,
    when I was woven together in the depths of the earth.
Your eyes saw my unformed body;
    all the days ordained for me were written in your book
    before one of them came to be.

PSALM 139:13-16

### Journal Prompts

1. Do you like being the kind of feeler God made you to be? Why or why not?

2. Which of the strengths listed in this chapter do you most relate to? How might you begin using those gifts more intentionally?

3. Describe a time when you have used your emotional disposition to help someone else. How did you feel afterward?

# CHAPTER 3

# THE HAPPY HOUSE

Flashback to several years ago (ahem, "several" meaning "more years ago than I care to admit"): I'm in my early twenties, a newlywed who is also newly employed and newly moved away from family. Away from my roots. Away from all that feels familiar and safe. Kevin is driving us home one night and I'm upset about something—maybe it's a surge of homesickness or a guilty conscience in my walk with God or the way I can never get the chicken to finish cooking at the same time as the vegetables—but whatever the reason, the feelings are flowing.

Kevin pulls the car into our driveway, and we sit there idling for a while. He listens and tries to help, but I somehow manage to bat away all his comforting words with my own discouraging ones. *It's not that simple; that doesn't make it go away; I don't feel any better.* At last he takes a deep breath and points to our snug brick rental home, its front porch lights twinkling a warm welcome. "You see that house?" he says, waiting till I look up.

I nod.

"That is the Happy House," he says. "And only happy people are allowed inside." He grins, softening the words so I know it's kind of a joke. "I know you need some time to yourself to pray and sort all *this*"—he wiggles his fingers in circles near my heart—"out, so I'll give you time. Now I'm going inside the Happy House, because I choose to be happy. We have each other, and God loves us. The world isn't perfect, but it's still a pretty great place, and I hope you'll take a minute to just pray, leave it all with God, and then come join me inside."

He leans in to kiss me on the forehead. I give a reluctant sniffle-snort in response and watch his tall frame walk into the house. *The Happy House,* I correct myself, rolling my eyes with an almost-smile.

Alone in the dark car, I ponder his words, his wisdom, his relentless optimism. I mumble my irritation. Joy seems so easy for him; why is it always so complicated for me?

My wiser-than-his-twentysomething-years husband had only just begun teaching me a lesson I am still working to embrace today: we can learn to put boundaries on our feelings. That's not to say that God expects us to be happy all the time or that we should stuff down negative feelings. But we don't have to let dark feelings dominate us, defeat us, define us. We can refuse to invite certain toxic emotions into our homes—or demand that they leave if they force their way inside. When we learn how to do that, any house can become a happy house.

## THE NOT-SO-HAPPY HOUSE—ER, TENT

Let's drop in on some family-life scenes from a fellow big feeler in Scripture: Sarah, the wife of Abraham (formerly Abram). Sarah (originally named Sarai) did not have an easy marital road. First her husband announced that a mysterious divinity had called them to move—leave their home, family, friends, everything—and go . . . somewhere. Final destination unknown. (Imagine *that* conversation over a cup of coffee one morning!)

Then God made a promise—a promise Sarah's heart must have been aching to hear after many years of barrenness: God would give Abraham a family—a family from Sarah's own womb—and their descendants would outnumber the stars (see Genesis 15:4-5).

From a human perspective, God was slow in fulfilling his word. A decade after leaving her homeland and family, Sarah had given up on God's promise:

> Sarai, Abram's wife, had borne him no children. But she had an Egyptian slave named Hagar; so she said to Abram, "The Lord has kept me from having children. Go, sleep with my slave; perhaps I can build a family through her."
>
> Abram agreed to what Sarai said.
>
> GENESIS 16:1-2

My writer's imagination loves filling in Bible scenes with color and context, so I envision this exchange going something like this:

> Sarah stands before Abraham in his tent. Her veil is lowered; her dark hair cascades around her rigid shoulders. "Abraham, the Lord has kept me from having children." Her words are cold, hard edged. Abraham opens his mouth to object, to remind her for the ten thousandth time of God's promise, his power, his faithfulness, but the bitter glint in Sarah's eye tells him the words will fall on deaf ears.
>
> Sarah tosses her hair over her shoulder. Without turning, she barks a command: "Hagar! Come in here."

A young maid scurries in to stand one step behind her mistress, head ducked in subservience, eyes on the woven rug at her feet.

"Go," Sarah says, waving a hand between Abraham and Hagar. "Make her a concubine. She is young enough"—the words twist bitterly through Sarah's age-lined lips—"and she should conceive quickly. Perhaps I can build a family through her."

Hagar's head snaps up. Her shocked eyes dart from mistress to master back to mistress before finding the rug once more. She knits her fingers together in a trembling knot.

Abraham rises to his feet, just as surprised as the slave girl. He blinks at Sarah for a moment, ready to object, to insist she wait just a little longer, but when he sees raw hope flickering in her eyes—a spark he has not seen in many long years—the words die in his throat.

He sighs and sits down again. "If this is really what you want."

"Yes." Sarah's voice rings triumphant, relieved. "This is what I want."

And of course things go south, as human plans that attempt to manipulate God's will always do. When Hagar learned she was pregnant, she grew arrogant, despising Sarah. I picture the Bible scene unfolding something like this:*

Sarah bursts into Abraham's tent, brushing the opening aside so roughly it rips.

Abraham jumps to his feet. "Sarah, what—"

Sarah raises a shaking finger and points it at Abraham.

---

* This story is found in Genesis 16:3-6. I drew as much dialogue as possible directly from Scripture.

"You! You did this to me! You are responsible for the wrong I am suffering."

Baffled, Abraham raises helpless palms. "I—my love, what are you talking about?"

"That—that girl. Hagar," Sarah spits out the name. "I put her in your arms, and now that she is with child, she despises me." Tears glitter in Sarah's eyes, and she swipes them away with a fist. "I am even more humiliated than I was before."

Abraham takes one step forward, wanting to draw his wife into his arms. "But my love, *you* are my—"

"Stop!" Sarah says, one hand up like a wall between them. "May the Lord judge between you and me."

Abraham feels defensive words bubble up inside. *This was your idea, not mine! I was just trying to make you happy!* But seeing the fury and hurt contorting his wife's face, he says nothing.

Sarah's chest heaves with the sobs she is fighting to hold inside. Abraham longs to comfort her, but he knows it's no use. Keeping his voice even, careful, he says, "The girl—the slave—is nothing to me. You know that."

When his wife looks up, lip quivering, he dares a small smile. "You are my sun and stars, Sarah. Always have been. Always will be." He sits back on his couch, rubbing a weathered hand across his face. "Your slave is in your hands. Do with her whatever you think best."

A dark smile flickers around Sarah's mouth. She spins on her heel and leaves the tent. Abraham's stomach knots. He doesn't want to know what Sarah has in mind.

We don't know exactly what happened next between these two women, but the Bible does tell us this: Sarah mistreated Hagar so badly that the pregnant concubine eventually risked her life to flee the abuse. She took her chances on surviving alone in the harsh wilderness rather than remaining in Sarah's care.

When I read this story, my heart aches for both women: Sarah, the wealthy woman so far from home, longing for a child before her aging arms were too weak to hold him; and Hagar, the slave turned concubine who must bear a child only to give him away.

I know what it is to wait for a child. To count days, month after bleeding month, empty womb aching. To wake, night after lonely night, soaking your pillow with tears as you plead with God until dawn. To feel hope rise in your traitorous heart even though your mind insists it's impossible, already too late. I know what that kind of desperation, the months and years of disappointment and heartache, can do to your faith. Your relationships. Even your personality.

We see hints of all the complex feelings and struggles that accompany Sarah's barrenness—the bitterness, the faithlessness, the desire to take control—in the person Sarah has become. Although you and I have some cultural distance from things like slavery and concubines, we can still relate to many of Sarah's feelings. Her experiences—even her mistakes—can point us to truth and insight. Because regardless of culture and circumstance, we all face emotionally charged difficulties at home and in our families.

## WHEN MAMA AIN'T HAPPY . . .

Let's start with big feelers. Big feelers tend to wield a lot of emotional influence at home. Our capacity for expressing affection and experiencing joy, coupled with our sympathetic nature, often makes us the person in our household who best connects with everyone else. When other people we live with—whether that's a spouse or a parent or children or siblings or roommates—are sad, they seek our sympathy. When they have a funny story to tell, they crave our laughter. When they've earned a victory, they call for our ecstatic celebration. In those times, what a gift our emotions can be to the people we love!

Of course, our strong emotions can have a dark side too. Because our moods are so strong, they tend to seep past our own internal boundaries and influence others. Some of us can't hide our feelings. When deep sadness descends upon us, its shadow may darken a room; when we are happy, our infectious joy can lift the whole household.

Growing up in the South, I often heard people say, "When Mama ain't happy, ain't nobody happy." Perhaps we could adapt the phrase to say, "When the big feeler ain't happy, ain't nobody happy." The opposite also holds true: "When the big feeler is happy, the whole house is happy!"

Our emotions are so expansive they can take up massive real estate, but we have to learn to share emotional space at home. In the account from Genesis, we see that Sarah's emotions—at least during the particular season of her marriage we just explored—dictated the course of her family life.* With Sarah despondent and desperate, Abraham, likely fearing his wife's sadness or anger, stepped aside and let Sarah have her way even though he knew it contradicted God's plan. Sadly, painful consequences followed for all involved, affecting their family for generations to come (see Genesis 16:11-12; 21:8-21).

What can we learn from this story? Certainly we can learn to trust God and not manipulate or take over even when we dislike his timing. But we can find another application: we have to pay special attention to how our emotions influence our home life. Let's learn from Sarah's struggles that we can't make our loved ones revolve around our emotions. Others have intense feelings

---

* At other times, it was Abraham's fears that guided them, while Sarah showed great courage (see Genesis 12 and 20).

too—we may be enduring a rough day or a rough season, but that doesn't mean other people aren't suffering too. Like attracts like, and we often live with other sensitive souls. If you're a parent, chances are you have a sensitive child who is very much like you, who is quietly reading and absorbing feelings—especially yours—from across the room. Two or more deep feelers under one roof can be a recipe for an intense household atmosphere!

As Proverbs 14:1 warns us, "The wise woman builds her house, but with her own hands the foolish one tears hers down." Whew. I know. That one's a heavy hitter. And yet what painful truth we find in those pointed words! If we don't pay attention to who we are at home, we are liable to tear down the families God has given us, hurting the people we love most: parents, siblings, children, spouses.

A year or so into my own struggle with infertility, I began to notice a change in my husband: his silly jokes ceased, his cheerful whistling fell silent. We shuffled past each other mumbling muffled greetings—our home gradually grew muted, as if we lived underwater. I felt myself slowly drowning beneath my sadness, and although Kevin had jumped into the water beside me, we were trapped, treading water in a powerful current, and neither of us knew the way back to shore.

One day, with a jolt of self-revelation, I realized that I had to find a way through this. I didn't know how the story would end. Would God ever say yes? Would we ever cradle a child in our arms? But I still had to *live*. As agonizing as this wait was, as bleak as our future felt, I still had an adoring husband whom I also adored, and we could still experience joy—even laughter—in the midst of heartache and uncertainty. I decided to do whatever it took to keep my head above water. I decided to fight. Baby steps at first: opening up to a few more trusted friends, begging God to help me notice and cling to small moments of joy, simply smiling at Kevin and asking him about his day. Then bigger steps: seeking purpose, finding ways to serve others, reclaiming this "lost" time for God.

## THE STRUGGLE IS REAL

Steady-feeler Kevin and big-feeler Elizabeth had a lot to learn in those years about how to live with our different emotional make-ups: how to guard against our weaknesses, share emotional space, and use our gifts to comfort each other. It's a lesson we continue to learn today. As long as we are in relationship with other people, we *all* have to learn how to live alongside other types of feelers.

While big feelers must choose to make room for others' emotions, steady feelers and reluctant feelers face different challenges. Reluctant feelers may need to accept the depth and intensity of others' emotions, recognizing that although they may not always relate to being overwhelmed by emotion, the struggle, as they say, is real. And deep feelers need that struggle to be acknowledged and embraced by the people closest to us—through conversation, prayer, and emotional support. So a word to you reluctant feelers: once others' feelings are out in the open, be prepared to offer your gifts of steadiness, logic, and peace as you comfort and counsel.

Reluctant feelers, keep in mind that while you may possess the ability to compartmentalize your emotions, other people may not work that way. Big-feeling types can't just muscle through their emotions, ignore them, or pack them away until a more convenient time. (Is there ever a convenient time for lots of feelings?) If they do, one day the closet door will burst open, unleashing an avalanche of junk that will bury any poor soul nearby. As the wise preacher at my wedding told my husband, "Two minutes now saves two hours later." In other words, it's better to invite the more sensitive types in your life to discuss and unpack small feelings day by day, rather than ignoring feelings in the hope that they'll fade over time.

Steady feelers, your temptation may be to grow frustrated with the feelers on either end of the spectrum. Why don't the big feelers hold it together? Why won't the reluctant feelers express their emotions? But steady feelers, the more you employ your gifts, the less frustrated you'll feel. You can use your capacity for emotional depth to deliberately draw out the emotions of the people around you. As Proverbs 20:5 puts it, "The purposes of a person's heart are deep waters, but one who has insight draws them out." You can prompt needed conversations by asking simple questions: "How are you feeling? What's really going on inside?" The reluctant feelers need the reminder to admit that they do, in fact, have feelings, and the big feelers need permission to air out their emotions, along with a safe place to do so. Once those emotions are expressed, perhaps you can serve as the translator between any extremes in your home, helping the big feelers to untangle their knotted emotions and helping the reluctant feelers to acknowledge their own feelings and empathize with the feelings of others.

I love the way the Bible describes how the famous "Proverbs 31 woman" sets a joyful mood in her home:

> She is clothed with strength and dignity;
>     she can laugh at the days to come.
> She speaks with wisdom,
>     and faithful instruction is on her tongue. . . .
> Her children arise and call her blessed;
>     her husband also, and he praises her:
> "Many women do noble things,
>     but you surpass them all."
> PROVERBS 31:25-26, 28-29

Strength. Dignity. Confidence for the future. This is the kind of woman I seek to become—not to give in to every swell of emotion, but to find strength in the constancy of God's Word and his promises. To be so confident in his care that I can laugh at the days to come. To give my family the incomparable gift of a cheerful, God-centered home, a safe haven from the world.

## INGREDIENTS FOR A HAPPY HOME

So what are the key ingredients in keeping your house happy—and emotionally healthy? In some ways this is a complex question, but ultimately it boils down to three words: selflessness, self-awareness, and self-control.

### Selflessness

When we are experiencing intense feelings, it can be difficult to look past our own emotions to notice and validate others' feelings. And yet God calls us to a life of selflessness. This isn't to suggest that we ignore our own feelings, of course, but we are *also* called to pay attention to others' needs. How wise our Creator is! How well he understands what makes us thrive. He designed us to give, and we are always happier and healthier when we do.

In one of God's beautiful paradoxes, selflessness is one of the best things we can do *for ourselves*! When I take my eyes off my own problems and moods in order to focus on meeting others' needs, I am always amazed at how my own problems seem smaller and my own emotional state improves. As Paul reminds us, selflessness is at the core of our faith:

> Never act from motives of rivalry or personal vanity, but in humility think more of each other than you do of yourselves. None of you should think only of his own affairs, but should learn to see things from other people's point of view.
> PHILIPPIANS 2:3-4, PHILLIPS

## Self-Awareness

Jesus' half-brother James encourages us to remain self-aware:

> Don't just listen to God's word. You must do what it
> says. Otherwise, you are only fooling yourselves. For if
> you listen to the word and don't obey, it is like glancing
> at your face in a mirror. You see yourself, walk away, and
> forget what you look like. But if you look carefully into
> the perfect law that sets you free, and if you do what it
> says and don't forget what you heard, then God will bless
> you for doing it.
>
> JAMES 1:22-25, NLT

Self-awareness saves our relationships! Emotion can be both blinding and distorting: it inflates our own sense of importance by magnifying our problems—not to mention magnifying the weaknesses of others. But when we are self-aware—mindful of our own tendencies, strengths, and weaknesses—we are able to keep our own concerns in a healthy perspective. Self-awareness allows us to make a more fair-minded evaluation of ourselves—and others. Self-awareness helps us remove the proverbial planks from our own eyes before pointing out infinitesimal specks in the eyes of the people we love (Matthew 7:3-5).

## Self-Control

Peter urges us to embrace self-control:

> Prepare your minds for action; be self-controlled; set
> your hope fully on the grace to be given you when Jesus
> Christ is revealed. . . . Therefore be clear minded and self-
> controlled so that you can pray.
>
> 1 PETER 1:13, 4:7

We exercise emotional self-control when we acknowledge and deal with our feelings, yet also give them godly boundaries. We exercise self-control when we protect our children or other vulnerable people from overhearing us unpack painful feelings, and when we take our hurt and anger to God rather than directing them toward the people we live with and love most.

* * *

Practically speaking, what do selflessness, self-awareness, and self-control look like at home? How might we apply these traits in everyday interactions with family members and roommates?

- We deliberately and consistently use our gifts of sensitivity and compassion to encourage, comfort, console, and uplift the people we live with.
- We remain self-aware when strong feelings arise. We exercise wisdom for when and how we communicate our feelings—not simply unpacking all our emotional baggage on the doormat the moment we get home.
- We don't disengage from people every time we face difficulty or a shifting mood.
- We exercise self-control with our behavior and words, careful not to jerk our loved ones around whenever our feelings fluctuate.
- We resist the temptation (and what a temptation it is!) to withdraw into our own thoughts and feelings. Instead, we make it a point to remain consistently interested and invested in the lives of the people we live with. We take our eyes off our own feelings to ask, "How are *you* doing? What's going on with *you*?"
- We choose joy when our loved ones need us to. Even on days when we don't *feel* joyful, we decide to be present

anyway. To engage. To listen. Even to laugh. To set aside our own burdens for the sake of the people we love.

- And perhaps most important, we apologize when we realize we've become self-focused. (And we *all* have moments when we lose ourselves in our own feelings.) Let us never underestimate the great power in two small words: "I'm sorry."

Selflessness, self-awareness, and self-control. I know embracing these qualities is much easier said than done—oh, how I know! We all face days when we allow the powerful undertow of our sensitivities to drag us under and hold us down. But we can fight to swim back to the surface and try again the next day. The effort is worth it. Worth praying about. Worth the extra effort on extra-emotional days. Because after salvation, a happy home is perhaps the greatest treasure God offers this side of heaven.

I shared about the anguish of our infertile years, the heartache that was so overwhelming for my big-feeling heart that I nearly drowned—and dragged Kevin under with me. But in time, with the power of the Spirit, the help of Scripture, the support of friends, and small victories over a million daily battles, I inched out of the riptide—closer to God, closer to hope, closer to Kevin. We returned to the smiles and laughter and joy we had once shared. Our home was different, yes—the bright colors of our joy were made richer and more nuanced by shadows—but we found our way out of the water. And one happy day, Kevin started whistling again.

Sarah, too, found new life—lasting joy—as an old woman. At the age of ninety, Sarah held her longed-for baby at last, sharing a chuckle with God as she named her son Isaac, meaning "he laughs." Our merciful God did not disqualify Sarah from his promise because her faith and feelings sometimes faltered. What a testament to the depth and breadth of his grace! Yes, Sarah's tents were unhappy for a time, but God brought laughter back to her home.

And some years later, when Sarah departed this world, her grieving son, Isaac, found a wife of his own, Rebekah. Where did Isaac choose to begin his new life with his bride? Where did he want to build a home with the woman he loved? Back in his mother's tent, the home where he had experienced so much joy as a boy:

> Isaac brought her into the tent of his mother Sarah, and he married Rebekah. So she became his wife, and he loved her; and Isaac was comforted after his mother's death.
>
> GENESIS 24:67

Now that's a happy ending. *That's* a happy house.

## FEELING YOUR WAY FORWARD

### Prayer Prompt

> How lovely is your dwelling place,
>    LORD Almighty!
> My soul yearns, even faints,
>    for the courts of the LORD;
> my heart and my flesh cry out
>    for the living God.
> Even the sparrow has found a home,
>    and the swallow a nest for herself,
> where she may have her young—
>    a place near your altar,
> LORD Almighty, my King and my God.
>    Blessed are those who dwell in your house;
>    they are ever praising you.
>
> PSALM 84:1-4

## Journal Prompts

1. What is the overarching mood in my home? What do I *want* my home to feel like?

2. Are most of the things you say negative or positive? Even in the midst of difficulty or discouragement, how can you deliberately speak about gratitude and joy?

3. Fill in the blank: When I share my emotions with people at home, I feel _____

   _____.

4. Big feelers: When you feel emotionally overwhelmed, how do you typically respond at home? (Some people withdraw into their own thoughts and feelings, becoming quiet and lost in thought; others explode all over the house; others use some combination of the two.) How would you *like* to respond? How can you give yourself time and space to recharge so you still have emotional energy to give at other times?

   Steady feelers: You likely spend a lot of time giving to others, but what would help you to feel like your emotional needs are being acknowledged at home? When you feel emotionally overwhelmed, how do you typically respond?

   Reluctant feelers: How can you help create a validating, welcoming environment that invites your more emotional loved ones to be open with you? How can you be intentional about sharing your feelings and emotionally engaging with others at home?

CHAPTER 4

# WHEN DARKNESS COMES KNOCKING

David lies facedown. Stone floor, dark room. Curtains drawn, stomach empty—but it has been empty so long he no longer feels hunger, only a vast hollowness.

At first the prayers were lengthy, eloquent. They had structure, logic, lyricism: *Oh, Lord, you are good. You do not blame children for the sins of their fathers. This is my sin, my responsibility, my fault. As a father has compassion on his children, so you have compassion on those who fear you. Have mercy, good Father. Be just, loving Lord.*

Between prayers, he painted the stone with tears, as if his eyes were bleeding. But as days slouched on with no improvement for the child and no food for the father, the prayers distilled down to the barest of words, the plainest of pleas: *Show mercy. Spare him. Take me.* His throat is dry, his lips are raw, he makes no sound. Even so, every breath is a prayer.

A knock at the door, a quiet call: "My lord king, I'm coming in." Then a sliver of light. He does not stir, does not lift his forehead from the floor. He hears the slide of metal against wood—the old, untouched food tray removed, a fresh, also-to-be-untouched tray delivered. A formality to ease the servants' minds so no one can say they starved the king of Israel.

As the door swings shut, David hears whispers, fragments: "Can't tell . . . do himself harm."

His heart plunges; his spent stomach twists in on itself. *It is finished. My boy is gone.*

He sits up and calls out in a voice raspy with disuse, "Is the child dead?"

The door cracks open; he squints in the harsh slice of daylight. A young man's face appears, silhouetted and hazy in the shine of day. David pushes the words out again: "Is the child dead?"

The servant licks his lips, looks behind him as if seeking rescue. "I—"

"Tell me!" David commands. His voice, usually authoritative, sounds weak.

A shuffling sound, harsh whispers; the servant's face disappears. The door flies open, as if the hand that pushed did not know its own strength. A grizzly face appears in a halo of light: Benaiah. Lion slayer, bodyguard, old friend.*

And David knows. They would not send Benaiah to deliver good news.

"Is the child dead?" David whispers. He knows, yet needs to hear the words.

Benaiah's eyes glint with tears, but he does not look

---

* See 1 Chronicles 11:22-25.

away. "Yes, my lord. The child is dead. He . . . he passed without pain."

The sound that claws its way out of David's chest is a growl, a groan, an animal in anguish. "Leave—me," he grunts. Benaiah twitches as if to step forward, but then bows and retreats. The first retreat of his life.

For long minutes David slumps silent on the floor. Praying without words. He stands on legs that hardly remember how. When the room stops spinning, he reaches for a water glass, takes careful sips. Limps to the door, raps three times. The door springs open before the third rap has even died.

"Yes, my lord?" An aging servant stands in the doorway. Her eyes are red-rimmed and creased with worry.

"Draw me a bath," he says. "I'm going to worship. When I return, I will want a meal."

Her pale lips fall open. "My lord—I—do you understand? Your son, sweet babe—"

"Is dead." The words fall like stones from David's mouth. "I understand."

She steps inside, twisting her fingers. "Forgive my boldness, my lord, but when the child was alive, you mourned and fasted; now that he is dead, you want to worship and feast?"

David rubs a hand across his face. Presses thumbs against the temples he now realizes are pounding. "While the child was alive, I fasted and wept. I thought, 'Who knows? The Lord may be gracious to me and let the boy live.' But now that he is dead, why should I carry on fasting? Can I bring him back again? I will go to him, but he will not return to me."

The servant nods, lips pressed together.

"Now draw my bath and bring my clothes. I must comfort the child's mother, and I cannot do so in sackcloth and ash."*

What a fascinating story about David, our kindred spirit in Scripture—not only the king of Israel, but also the king of deep feelings. David's example offers insights into the life of a deeply emotional person who walks with God even after horrific spiritual collapse. After committing adultery and murder, David repented and pleaded with God to spare the life of the illegitimate son who was born to Bathsheba, his mistress. But when the child died, David got up, worshiped God, ate a meal, went to comfort Bathsheba—and baffled his servants with his seemingly callous behavior.

Not long after the death of their son, David and Bathsheba (now married) had another baby, another boy: Solomon. I wonder how Solomon felt about the older brother he never got to meet. Perhaps the dead brother was a shadow haunting Solomon's growing-up years: the two-paces-faster boy who should have run wild with Solomon through palace corridors; the one-head-taller boy who should have taught his little brother to slide sock-footed down smooth hallway floors, then come running to comfort—and maybe tease—when he fell.

I imagine David pulling young Solomon onto his knee, telling him their family's tragic tale. Teaching him about redemption and healing after sin and death. I picture David hugging Solomon close, inhaling his little-boy smell of wheat and sunshine, whispering into his dark curls, "I had to get up again. Live again. Love again. You, my boy, were my grace, my healing, my light at night's end. You were the joy in the morning. You brought the dawn."

---

*Based on 2 Samuel 12:14-25.

All grown up, Solomon wrote a book of wisdom, and he penned these immortal words, perhaps remembering the brother he never knew:

There is a time for everything,
>    and a season for every activity under the heavens:

>    a time to be born and a time to die . . .
>    a time to weep and a time to laugh,
>    a time to mourn and a time to dance . . .
>    a time to embrace and a time to refrain from embracing,
>    a time to search and a time to give up. . .
>    a time to be silent and a time to speak.

ECCLESIASTES 3:1-2, 4-7

When Solomon composed his poem, he was gently echoing, perhaps unconsciously, lyrics his father had written to be sung at the dedication of the Temple:

His anger lasts only a moment,
>    but his favor lasts a lifetime;
weeping may stay for the night,
>    but rejoicing comes in the morning . . .
You turned my wailing into dancing;
>    you removed my sackcloth and clothed me with joy.

PSALM 30:5, 11

Solomon learned a powerful lesson about loss, just as his father had: we may weep for a night—even a season of nights—but joy comes with the dawn. There is a time for everything—and a season for every feeling. Much as we may hate the dark feelings, much as we may long to avoid them, even the dark feelings have their place.

As one who has spent a lifetime trying to outrun the shadows, I find Solomon's truth strangely relieving:

There *is* a time to mourn.
There *is* a time to weep.
And there *is* a time to let go.

Grief is not evil. At least not inherently so. Not all the time. Sure, some grief is misplaced; some sorrow lasts too long; some regret lingers and harms; some guilt is unnecessary. But we don't need to avoid all dark feelings all the time, at all costs. Many painful feelings serve a God-given purpose, and when we try to stifle them, we suffer consequences.

And let us remember: God himself grieves—and he is perfect. Jesus grieves too—"man of sorrows," Isaiah calls him. If God Almighty has experienced grief, then we don't need to feel bad when we endure a season of grief. We don't need to berate ourselves when our lives take a turn for the dark. We don't need to feel like we're sinful or like something is wrong with us.

All the feelings we experience—even the difficult ones—were given to us by God to help us experience, process, and learn from every facet of life. If we couldn't feel guilt when we sinned, how would we ever grow? If we didn't experience regret when we made mistakes, how could we ever learn? If we were incapable of grief when someone died, how could we ever heal?

Grief, guilt, and sorrow are necessary. They serve a purpose. And when we experience them in a healthy way, they are good— the doorway to healing. Yes, we may limp through the door still bearing scars, but the passing-through binds the bleeding and starts the healing.

Steady feelers and reluctant feelers, although this advice may go against your instinct, I encourage you not to lock the dark feelings out of your heart when their time has come. Yes, you may delay their visit, but not for long. If you do, you'll end up with a persistent visitor who won't. Stop. Knocking. The longer you hold the bolt in place, the larger the grief outside will grow—it might even gather a few new friends: guilt, regret, bitterness. When the posse of pain finally knocks your door off its hinges, it'll overrun the house.

And when sorrow pays a visit to people you love, don't be afraid to keep vigil with them. To *let them hurt* without feeling pressure to fix their pain, abbreviate it, or minimize it.

Sometimes big-feeling types feel sad *because* we feel sad, or guilty *because* we feel guilty—a circular, counterproductive, self-defeating cycle. As David and Solomon teach us, dark feelings are a natural, inescapable part of life here on earth. Only in heaven will God wipe away the tears, the reasons for tears, perhaps even the memory of tears (see Isaiah 25:7-8; 51:10-11).

I spent many years of my life assuming that depression and guilt and sorrow and any emotion that felt negative should be avoided as much as possible. (And of course, as a big feeler, such feelings often hounded me . . . which left me feeling all the more discouraged, guilty, and unspiritual.) But in recent years, I have changed my mind. I'm learning that sometimes—not all the time, but sometimes—when darkness comes knocking, I need to open the door and let it in.

The trick is learning when it's time to usher a particular dark feeling back out. When to declare the visit at an end, to stand at the door saying, "Here's your hat; what's your hurry?" We need to know when it's time to shoo it out so we can make room for other, happier feelings. To know when it's time to laugh. Time to dance. Time to embrace.

The problem, of course, is that the dark feelings like to overstay their welcome. And sometimes they show up for no reason.

## A KNOCK IN THE NIGHT

A blistering wail pierces the night. My parents jolt upright in bed, hearts slamming against their ribs. The clock blinks 3:00 a.m. in unforgiving red numbers. Mom and Dad sit squinting at each other, doubting their own ears. Did something happen? Was there a noise?

Another scream: a muffled wail. Then the doorbell rings, and small thumps sound on the front door. The door underneath the window to my little brothers' second-story bedroom.

Mom gasps. "Dear God, oh, the boys—the window—"

But Dad doesn't hear her—he's already gone, flying down two flights of stairs in two kamikaze leaps. He flings open the door, bracing himself to see a broken body on the front doorstep. Which son would it be?

A small boy in airplane pajamas stands shrieking on the front mat, fists clenched, eyes wide. Dad gapes at him for a moment, then flips on a light. "Liam?" he asks, recognizing the three-year-old from three houses down. The angry house, the house with all the shouting. "Liam, honey, are you all right?"

But Liam only screams—garbled, wordless. Dad kneels down, searching for injury, for blood.

Mom skids to a stop behind Dad. "Liam?" she pants. "Oh, baby, what's wrong?" She bends down, scooping him up in her arms. He curls into her, whimpering.

Mom turns to Dad, fear in her eyes. "Sammy, you'd better go down there. You don't think his parents . . . ?" She can't say the words, but Dad knows what she means.

His expression is grim. He grabs a baseball bat from behind the door. "Wait by the phone. If I'm not back in five minutes, call the police."

Dad sprints down the dark street to Liam's house, expecting to find the front door open and domestic disturbance brewing inside. But the door is shut. The house stands dark.

It takes three minutes of pounding and ringing before Liam's father opens the door, bleary eyed. "Are you okay, Ralph?" Dad clenches the bat nervously. "Liam is at our house, and he's screaming."

"We're fine." Ralph's eyes zero in on the bat. "Wait, what? Liam is where?"

\* \* \*

It was days before Mom and Dad could tell this story without twitching. Turns out little Liam was a sleepwalker, and he'd climbed out of bed and wandered through our neighbors' front yards to our house, apparently dreaming about asking my brothers to come out to play. But then when he got to our door, he woke up, disoriented and terrified.

I tell this story from my childhood because sometimes, like poor Liam, big feelings come pounding on our doors, and they don't really have a purpose. We aren't sure how they got there, or why. Some days we wake up and we're just sad. For no identifiable reason. Life is the same as it was yesterday; our relationships are all fine—or at least as fine as they were yesterday. No Big Bad Thing has happened—we just feel *down*. Sadness and anxiety have come calling, and they're standing on the doorstep, hoping we will let them in.

In times when I can find no apparent reason for my dark feelings, I find it helpful to take written inventory. I like to sit down with God and paper and pen and ask myself a few searching questions, similar to the ones my parents asked Liam:

Did something bad happen?
Are you anxious about something in particular?
Do you feel unresolved in a conflict with someone?
Have you committed a sin you feel guilty about?

Sometimes my investigations turn up something I need to deal with—an explanation for the feelings, an issue I can address through prayer and conversation. But other times, I find nothing. The answer to all four questions is no. The feelings may *feel* real, but they have no real cause. It's then I realize I've got a sleepwalker at my door. And there's only one thing to do with sleepwalkers: send them on their way. Once my parents realized little Liam was okay, they took the boy home where he belonged, where his own parents could tuck him into his own bed. (And add a few extra locks on the doors, out of three-year-old reach!)

When we feel sad for no clear reason or anxious without cause, we are under no obligation to hang out with those feelings long term. We have no obligation to invite them into our homes or our hearts.

To help the dark feelings on their way, I find it helpful to write down words of truth and repeat them to myself until the feelings gradually give up and stop knocking. In moments of emotional confusion, I cling to simple thoughts like these:

God loves me.
God has given me life.
God is taking care of me.
My feelings aren't telling the truth: I may feel sad, but I don't
    have to stay sad. I may feel anxious, but I don't have to
    stay anxious.
There are days to be unhappy, but today is not one of them.
There are days to be anxious, but today is not one of them.

These statements sound banal, I know, but that's the whole point. Just as poor barely awake Liam could only grasp the most basic of statements, so wild feelings respond best to simple realities.*

---

* Hang with me . . . we'll get to the feelings that won't take no for an answer—the ones that force their way inside.

## A KNOCK IN THE MORNING

My husband and I stand outside my parents' kitchen door (a different door than the door of Liam fame), and we can hardly contain our excitement . . . or the wriggling puppy in Kevin's arms.

We tap quietly and peer into the sleepy kitchen with sheepish grins. "I hope we don't scare them to death," I whisper to Kevin.

"If we do, it's your fault," Kevin whispers back. "This was your idea." I stick out my tongue at him and knock again.

My mother shuffles to the door in her robe, a cup of coffee in hand, confusion on her face. "Seven a.m.?" is all she manages.

"Morning, Mom," I say, darting in to drop a kiss on her cheek. "I hope we didn't scare you."

Mom finds her smile and her voice, stepping back and pulling the door wide, waving us inside. "Of course not. Oh!" Her eyes land on the black fur ball writhing in Kevin's arms behind me. "Is this the new Thompson?"

"Yes!" I reach back to scratch his floppy ears. He slimes my hand with puppy slobber.

My little sister Alexandra, the only child still living at home, rushes into the kitchen, shoving papers into her backpack. "Mom, I need five dollars for—" She stops and lets out a squeal, her silver braces gleaming. "The puppy!" She rushes over to squish his floppy cheeks between her hands. He pants and squirms with glee.

"We wanted to tell you his name before you left for school," I say. "Go get Dad and we'll tell you all together."

My sister tilts her head sideways, searching me through slitted eyes. "You are *really* excited about this puppy's name."

"Yep." I smile as non-mysteriously as I can. Alexandra shrugs— as if to say, *Whatever, grown-ups are weird*—and runs to get Dad.

When Dad yawn-smiles his way across the room, I hug him. "Sorry to show up unannounced, but we wanted you to meet the puppy and tell you his name. It's more fun in person—er, in puppy." My family offers us polite, if somewhat bewildered, smiles. "Cole! His name is Cole," I say, proudly. "And he has a Christmas birthday, so it's like we got *Cole* in our stocking. Get it?"

My family makes noises of approval and crowds in to welcome the newest and most slobbery family member. Kevin speaks over the hubbub: "We probably shouldn't have gotten a puppy right now, but we figured this way he'll be fully trained by the time the baby comes in December."

My mom, ever accommodating, ever eager to fill conversational gaps with happy words, coos, "Oh, yes, that will be gr—wait, whaaaa—?"

My sister claws at my arm, her hazel eyes wide and hopeful. "Are you—Did he say—"

"Baby?" Mom squeaks, then screams. "Did he say *baby*?"

Dad stands frozen, blinking.

I nod, grinning so big my face hurts. "Yes! Baby! I'm pregnant."

Dad shouts, punches a fist in the air, picks me up and whirls me around the kitchen. So much screaming, so much crying, so much joy. Three years' worth of screaming and crying and joy, all bottled up for release in these precious early-morning moments.

\* \* \*

That morning, that once-in-a-lifetime morning after what felt like a lifetime of mourning, Kevin and I showed up on my parents' doorstep with a lot of feelings in tow, and that day our feelings had a purpose. We were bearing joy (not to mention a baby . . . and a puppy). We were bringing change. News. A new season.

Some feelings come knocking for a reason. Sometimes we open the door to big joys, other times to big hurts. Either way, those big feelings, the legitimate ones, can't just be left standing on the doorstep. They can't be sent home with the neighbors. They have to be acknowledged, addressed, invited inside. And then discussed, examined, processed, experienced.

## THIS IS MY HOUSE

Maybe if we can change the way we think about dark feelings, we won't be so afraid of them. And maybe if we aren't so afraid, they won't hold so much power over us. They won't feel like intruders determined to break into our homes, ravage our hearts and our families, and place us on house arrest.

As eight-year-old Kevin McCallister says in the iconic movie *Home Alone*, "I can't be a wimp. I'm the man of the house!" Perhaps a new way of thinking can give us a greater sense of emotional control, the knowledge that we get to stand at the door and decide which feelings come in, and when. Just because they show up doesn't mean they get to unpack their bags for an indefinite stay. Maybe their purpose is important and they need to come in, but even so, we can decide when it's time for them to leave. As Kevin said, "This is my house. I have to defend it!"

But it's not always that easy, not always that straightforward, is it? We sometimes struggle with knowing when dark feelings have accomplished their purpose, when they are in danger of wearing out their welcome and need to be shown the door and sent on their way.

A time for everything.

A season for all things.

When we hear a knock on the door of our hearts, we need to ask some questions:

Which season am I supposed to be living right now?

Mourning or dancing? Weeping or laughing?

How long should that season last?

Are the feelings here for a good reason? Is this their time to
visit, or did they come to the wrong house?

These are not always easy questions to answer. Dark feelings
can come calling at our door daily, hourly, minute by minute. And
sometimes it's not just one dark feeling but a whole posse, with
torches and swords, threatening to burn the house down. They
won't be turned away no matter what we say or how we pray.

In those times, thank God he has provided outside help:
friends, therapists, mentors, counselors, and medicine. Depression
and anxiety are no laughing matter, and they can be crippling.
Overwhelming. Isolating. If dark feelings are knocking too often
at your door, or if they have already forced their way into your
home and unpacked for a long visit—perhaps even taken the
whole house hostage—I encourage you to call in reinforcements.
Seek whatever help you need. Call in the SWAT team, if that's
what it takes.

But in the meantime, don't stop putting in the work in your
head and heart. Don't stop developing mental tools and a scriptural
arsenal to bolster your ability to resist, to reinforce the strength of
the door to your heart. Don't stop learning how to help yourself even as you seek help from others. Whether or not you are
receiving outside care and counsel, you will need a multipronged
attack, and I hope this book provides some additional strategies
and Scriptures you can add to your personal toolbox.

Whatever feelings may be knocking on our hearts' doors today,
let us live unafraid. Let's keep the door hinges oiled, ready not just
to slam shut against the night with its gloom, but to swing open
to welcome the joyful feelings when daylight returns.

Let's live daring to be emotionally engaged rather than always
fearing the darkness. As David and Solomon taught us, there is a
time for everything, a season for every feeling. Not just mourning,

not just wailing, not just refraining . . . but also dancing, singing, embracing. Living life to the full. Feeling all the feels, both the dark and the light.

## FEELING YOUR WAY FORWARD

### Prayer Prompt

How lovely is your dwelling place,
   Lord Almighty!
My soul yearns, even faints,
   for the courts of the Lord;
my heart and my flesh cry out
   for the living God.
Even the sparrow has found a home,
   and the swallow a nest for herself,
   where she may have her young—
a place near your altar,
   Lord Almighty, my King and my God.
Blessed are those who dwell in your house;
   they are ever praising you.

PSALM 84:1-4

### Journal Prompts

1. How does it change your experience of dark feelings to realize that some painful feelings are necessary for a season?

2. How can you tell the difference between healthy grief and unhealthy grief?

3. How can you tell when dark feelings have overstayed their welcome?

# CHAPTER 5

# I CAN'T HELP THE WAY I FEEL
## . . . OR CAN I?

The police officer taps on the car window, and the redheaded driver, a man in his late twenties, rolls it down. The moment the window cracks open, a piercing wail blasts into the night, so loud the officer takes a step back. Peering into the backseat, the cop sees a red-faced young girl—she can't be more than three—sobbing so hard she's gasping for breath. The girl's mother sits beside her, stroking her arm.

"Uh, license and registration, please," the officer stammers. "You were going a little fast there."

"Yeah," mumbles the driver. "Sorry. Just wanted to get my daughter home." He fumbles through his wallet and the glove compartment and finally produces the documents. The wailing climbs an octave, and both men flinch.

"What's wrong with your daughter?" the officer asks, examining the license through squinty eyes. "Is she—is she afraid of policemen?" He stumbles over his words, as if he feels guilty.

"No . . . we took her to the movies," the father says, his mystified expression seeming to say, *We were trying to be good parents.*

The cop raises an eyebrow. "Did she fall down on the way out or something?"

"No." The father presses the heels of his hands against his forehead. "She thought the ending was sad."

At this, the child's wails reach a pitch usually only attainable by dog whistles and teakettles.

The officer grimaces. "You know what?" He thrusts the license and papers back through the window. "Just get that poor kid home. And drive more slowly this time."

Mumbling a sheepish "Thanks," the father pulls away, not bothering to roll up the window. The child's weeping trails the car like a siren.

\*     \*     \*

The story of "The Time I Cried So Hard I Got My Parents Out of a Speeding Ticket" has become legend in my family. I used to joke that the episode might have been one of the few times my—er, *intense*—emotions were demonstrably beneficial. It was certainly indicative of many feelings to come.

Strong emotion is a huge part of the big feeler's experience of the world. But intense feelings aren't just for big feelers; steady feelers and reluctant feelers are acquainted with them too. Although some people experience strong feelings more frequently than others, big feelings come knocking on everyone's door at some point.

Can we take a step back for a moment to address the unreliability of feelings? They can be influenced by a bizarre array of factors: last night's taco and this morning's coffee, the phase of the moon and the presence of pets. Feelings are not always a reliable indicator of truth or reality. And we all have to learn how to evaluate emotions: which are God honoring, which are not; which are healthy, which are not. We also have to learn how to categorize and manage feelings: which to encourage, which to avoid.

And that leads us to an all-important question, one we must answer before we can move on to more practical matters: *Can* we manage our feelings? And to be more specific, can we go so far as to avoid or limit specific feelings? Do we have any say in which emotions we experience or how intensely we experience them?

I say yes. We have a choice in how we think, and since our thoughts affect our emotions, we have a choice in how we feel.

Okay, time out. If you are a big feeler, you may be feeling a lot of things right now: hurt, defensive, even angry. *Ugh, here we go with more of that "choose joy" messaging everyone's always trying to shove down my throat. I can't help being so sensitive—I'm just wired like this! My feelings do what they want. If I* could *stop all these emotions, I totally* would. *And now I feel guilty on top of everything else!*

My friend, all I can say is, *I feel you.* Seriously. The concept of emotional choice is a tender topic for tender people like us.

But stay with me while we hash this out biblically and practically. I'm not trying to guilt-trip you for having wayward feelings, nor do I wish to stymie you with impossible standards or shallow "Give me two minutes, I'll give you absolute joy" promises. I don't mean to make light of hard times and dark thoughts. But even so, we can all seek to grow emotionally—to add new Scriptures, strategies, and convictions to our emotional toolbox.

So back to our question: *Can* we choose how we feel? Do we have any control over our sensitivities and emotions?

First, let me tell you a little of my story. You already met three-year-old me, who had zero control over her feelings; now let's meet teenage and twentysomething me.

## GETTING OUT OF THE FUNKS

After the Movie Incident, I grew older and a bit more self-controlled, though I learned to avoid sad movies. Especially sad movies involving dogs. But big feelings were still a constant companion. Sometimes those big feelings were joyful, sing-in-the-rain-and-twirl-with-your-umbrella-like-the-old-movies feelings, but then there were the other ones.

When I was in high school and college, I used to succumb to cloudy moods my family affectionately called "funks." I would disappear into my own dark feelings for a few days, either walking around the house Eeyore style, trailing my own personal rain cloud, or cocooning in my room, waiting for the sun to reappear. Looking back on those times, my funks weren't so much true depressive episodes as they were a combination of normal teenage hormones, growing pains, an overactive conscience, and (cough) an occasional flair for the dramatic.

Fast-forward a few more years . . . it was one thing to get "funky" when I was a single woman living in my own room, when the only person deeply affected by my emotional state was me. But then I married Kevin Thompson, aka Mr. Whistle-While-You-Work-and-Add-a-Few-Dance-Moves-While-You're-at-It-Because-Everything-Is-Awesome. A few months into our marriage, I indulged in a few funks (one of which you read about in chapter 3). My happy husband was bewildered by his new wife. He assumed that my being unhappy in general was my being unhappy with him, and bless him, he set about trying to fix me. As time wore on, his dance moves slowed; his whistling quieted.

When I saw what was happening to Kevin, and to my marriage, I realized with a shock of clarity that it was time for me to mature emotionally. To grow spiritually. To learn how to be intentional, consistent, and God-reliant in addressing my thoughts and moods. It was time to take advantage of Scripture, prayer, friend-ships, and the other tools God has given his people. I couldn't just roll over and say "uncle" every time cloudy feelings came calling; I had to deliberately seek the sun.

## WHAT *DOES* THE BIBLE SAY ABOUT FEELINGS?

Let's take a look at what the Bible has to say about emotions. We've already touched on some of Solomon's and David's writings about how all emotions—even the dark ones—have their proper place and time. We should also note that the Bible doesn't say things like, "When you're feeling depressed, try these three spiritual steps to change your mood." Rather, Scripture offers a more compre-hensive approach, addressing our mind-sets *and* our emotions.

Here are a few observations about how the Bible guides our emotional life:

- When addressing emotions, the Bible uses words like *heart, attitude, mind, spirit,* and *self-control.*
- The Bible discourages certain emotions—worry, jealousy, rage, and ungodly anger (to name a few)—and encourages others: patience, joy, peace, and righteous indignation (among many more).
- People in the Bible, many of them deeply emotional, displayed the full gamut of human emotion, and their stories provide examples of how God wants us to handle our emotions—and how he doesn't want us to handle them.
- When giving practical instructions, the Bible focuses more on directing our thoughts and our mind-sets than on modifying our feelings.

Let's ponder that last point for a moment: *The Bible focuses more on directing our thoughts and our mind-sets than on modifying our feelings.* If you really think about it, isn't that a relief? (If you've ever had someone tell you, "Just stop being sad! Get happy!" you may have had to restrain your foot from taking aim at their shin!) It just doesn't work to assume we can flip a switch to change our emotions.

Let's look at some examples of God's approach:

> We demolish arguments and every pretension that sets itself up against the knowledge of God, and we take captive every thought to make it obedient to Christ.
>
> 2 CORINTHIANS 10:5

> You were taught, with regard to your former way of life, to put off your old self, which is being corrupted by its deceitful desires; to be made new in the attitude of your minds; and to put on the new self, created to be like God in true righteousness and holiness.
>
> EPHESIANS 4:22-24

> Rejoice in the Lord always. I will say it again: Rejoice! . . . Do not be anxious about anything, but in everything, by prayer and petition, with thanksgiving, present your requests to God. And the peace of God, which transcends all understanding, will guard your hearts and your minds in Christ Jesus. Finally, brothers, whatever is true, whatever is noble, whatever is right, whatever is pure, whatever is lovely, whatever is admirable—if anything is excellent or praiseworthy—think about such things. . . . And the God of peace will be with you.
>
> PHILIPPIANS 4:4, 6-9

The Bible indicates that righteousness (not to mention peace!) follows when we *set our minds* on the things of God. And what kinds of things does God encourage us to focus on? Positive things! True, noble, right, pure, lovely, admirable, excellent, praiseworthy things. And when we set the attitude of our minds in a godly direction, godly feelings are far more likely to follow. Our *feelings* follow our *focus*.

It turns out there's a psychological term for this biblical exercise—it's called cognitive therapy. Dr. David Burns describes cognitive therapy and the science behind it in his book *Feeling Good: The New Mood Therapy*:

> A cognition is a thought or perception. In other words, your cognitions are the way you are thinking about things at any moment, including this very moment. These thoughts scroll across your mind automatically and often have a huge impact on how you feel. . . . Your feelings result from the messages you give yourself. In fact, your thoughts often have much more to do with how you feel than what is actually happening in your life. . . .
>
> The first principle of cognitive therapy is that *all* your moods are created by your "cognitions," or thoughts. A cognition refers to the way you look at things—your perceptions, mental attitudes, and beliefs. It includes the way you interpret things—what you say about something or someone to yourself. You *feel* the way you do right now because of the *thoughts you are thinking at this moment*. . . .
>
> The second principle is that when you are feeling depressed, your thoughts are dominated by a pervasive negativity. You perceive not only yourself but the entire world in dark, gloomy terms. What is even worse—you'll come to believe things *really are* as bad as you imagine them to be.[1]

We can clearly see the thought-feeling connection at work in the poetry of Jeremiah. Jeremiah, a sensitive soul known as the "weeping prophet," wrote heartbreaking commentary on the fall of Jerusalem and the plight of the Jews. His book Lamentations reads like a eulogy of sorts for his home and his people. In a series of laments, Jeremiah writes,

> I have been deprived of peace;
>> I have forgotten what prosperity is.
> So I say, "My splendor is gone
>> and all that I had hoped from the LORD."
>
> I remember my affliction and my wandering,
>> the bitterness and the gall.
> I well remember them,
>> and my soul is downcast within me.
>
> *Yet this I call to mind*
>> *and therefore I have hope:*
> Because of the LORD's great love we are not consumed,
>> for his compassions never fail.
> They are new every morning;
>> great is your faithfulness.
>
> *I say to myself,* "The LORD is my portion;
>> therefore I will wait for him."
>
> LAMENTATIONS 3:17-24 (EMPHASIS ADDED)

Do you see it—the connection between Jeremiah's thoughts and his mood? At first, he said to himself, "My splendor is gone and all that I had hoped from the LORD." His negative thoughts led to sad memories: affliction and wandering, bitterness and gall.

But notice the change in verse 21: "Yet this I call to mind and therefore I have hope: Because of the LORD's great love we are not consumed, for his compassions never fail. They are new every morning." The moment Jeremiah shifted his focus to the love and compassion of God, his mood shifted. Hope returned.

He continued this new train of thought: "I say to myself, 'The LORD is my portion; therefore I will wait for him.'" And now we see an attitude of greater fortitude and even contentment; we sense that Jeremiah was already finding the courage and perseverance to wait for God's salvation.

Choosing a new set of thoughts—God-centered thoughts, faithful thoughts—had a dramatic effect on how Jeremiah felt. His problems didn't go away, but now he had hope, because his eyes—and his mind—were back where they belonged: on God.

## WE DON'T HAVE TO BE VICTIMS

So how might these principles apply to us as we seek godly guidance for our thoughts and emotions? We can use Scripture to point us to the kind of thinking God wants us to have. We can be intentional about focusing the way we think, retraining our thought patterns to more closely follow God's paths.

Of course, this doesn't guarantee immediate, permanent relief from unwanted feelings, but it does help. And the more we deliberately work on our thoughts, the more we intentionally reframe negative thoughts, the better we will feel over time.

Again, let's listen to Dr. Burns:

Bad things do happen, and life beats up on most of us at times. Many people do experience catastrophic losses and confront devastating personal problems. Our genes, hormones, and childhood experiences probably do have an impact on how we think and feel. And other people can be annoying, cruel, or thoughtless. But all these theories about the causes of our bad moods have the tendency to make us victims—because we think the causes result from something beyond our control. After all, there is little we can do to change the way people drive at rush hour, or the way we were treated when we were young, or our genes or body chemistry (save taking a pill). In contrast, you can learn to change the way you think about things, and you can also change your basic values and beliefs. And when you do, you will often experience profound and lasting changes in your mood, outlook, and productivity. . . . The theory is straightforward and may even seem overly simple—but don't write it off as pop psychology.[2]

We can't anticipate perfect bliss or a personality overhaul—our struggles with sad or anxious feelings won't vanish the moment we experiment with a few positive thoughts. But we can anticipate growth, knowing that as we learn to think the way God wants us to think, our feelings will improve. Again, our *feelings* will follow our *focus*. In time, we can see significant forward progress. True change. More joy.

If we deliberately follow the thought patterns listed in Philippians 4:8, for example, our moods can't help but improve.

Why not test this idea now? Take five minutes and fill your mind with a few of the types of thoughts Paul suggests:

- Pure things: the laughter of children, a hug from a friend
- Excellent things: a heart-tugging song, a favorite meal
- Praiseworthy things: the strength of old trees, the light from God's stars

Try writing down a few specific examples and reading them over a few times. Now . . . how do you feel?

Do you see what I mean? After just a few moments spent focused on positive things—all gifts from God—you feel a little better, don't you? Imagine if we trained our thoughts to think this way most of the time! How differently might we feel—and live?[3]

## THE TWENTY-MINUTE RULE

As you work on your thinking, keep in mind that our emotions don't switch on and off like light bulbs. (*I'm feeling down, so I'll spend a few minutes praying, and the moment I say "amen" I'll feel happy!*) I like to keep in mind what my dad calls the Twenty-Minute Rule. Our brains and stomachs operate on a twenty-minute delay, meaning that when you eat, it may take you about twenty minutes to feel full. (Hence the sudden I-feel-like-I-just-ate-a-whole-watermelon stomachache you get whenever you inhale your food too fast!)

The principle in Dad's Twenty-Minute Rule applies to our emotions, too: After you pray and reset your thinking, don't expect immediate relief; give your emotions at least twenty minutes to catch up to your prayers and decisions. I know it sounds simplistic, and it may not always apply when monster-sized feelings come calling, but I encourage you to keep it in mind as you seek daily peace and joy. The Twenty-Minute Rule helps me stick to my decisions and not get discouraged when emotional relief comes more slowly than I think it should.

## THE POWER OF PAPER

One of the most effective methods I've found to wrangle and reframe my wayward thoughts is to put them down on paper. When I'm struggling, my dark thoughts often spin too fast and wild for me to catch, much less tame. They all swirl together into a tangled knot until I can't tell where one worry ends and another begins. But when I pluck the ball of thoughts out of my head, sort it into single threads, and put each thought on paper, I see more clearly.

Over the years, I have learned to make lists. Here are a few examples:

- Things I am worried about
- What God can do about the things I'm worried about
- Reasons I feel sad/guilty/insecure
- Ways I've seen God take care of me this week/this month/ this year
- Things I'm thinking that are true vs. things I'm thinking that aren't true
- Three Scriptures that remind me who God is
- Three things to be grateful for today
- Three ways I saw God show up today
- Three of God's promises I can praise him for today

Lists like these are simple but powerful tools that help emotion submit to logic and truth.[4]

## "SENSITIVE" DOESN'T MEAN "SAD"

All of this means that you're not a helpless prisoner to emotions, a victim with no say in how you think or feel. Although we all fight some mental and emotional battles—perhaps more frequent battles, if you're a big feeler—we aren't doomed to a life of unremitting mental torment and emotional anguish. Though we will all undergo rainy seasons, we need not live forever under clouds.

And if you're not a big feeler yourself, please don't get the wrong idea about us sensitive souls. We're not all angst and gloom— in fact, we are capable of abundant joy. In her book *The Highly Sensitive Person*—an enlightening, affirming read for sensitive souls and those who love them—Elaine Aron observes,

> When HSPs [Highly Sensitive People] react more
> [emotionally], it is as much or more to positive emotions,

such as curiosity, anticipation of success . . . , a pleasant desire for something, satisfaction, joy, and contentedness. Perhaps everyone reacts strongly to negative situations, but maybe HSPs . . . especially relish a good outcome and figure out more than others how to make it happen.[5]

Did you hear that? Sure, sensitive souls react to negativity, but we react *even more strongly* to positivity. If we can put in the work to "take captive" negative thoughts (2 Corinthians 10:5), and either reframe or replace them with the kinds of thoughts God calls us to have, not only can we avoid sad feelings, but we can experience unsurpassed joy.

Now *there's* a thought worth pondering!

## FEELING YOUR WAY FORWARD

### Prayer Prompt

May these words of my mouth
and this meditation of my heart
be pleasing in your sight,
Lord, my Rock and my Redeemer.

PSALM 19:14

### Journal Prompts

1. Create a list of your own by choosing one of the ideas mentioned on page 78 ("Things I am worried about," "What God can do about the things I'm worried about," "Three ways I saw God show up today," etc.).

2. Write down all the adjectives in Philippians 4:8 (true, noble, right, etc.), and make your own list of things that fit each adjective. Thank God for everything on your list, and deliberately spend time thinking about those blessings.

# CHAPTER 6

# FACTS VERSUS FEELINGS

Lisa steps into the warm café, stamping slush off her boots. The smoky smell of coffee curls around her. She savors the aroma even as she fights a twinge of sadness: the coffee smell is going to seep into her hair and replace the New Haircut Smell.

A quick glance around the café—no Gabriela. Lisa steps to the side, pulls out her phone, and uses the camera as a mirror. Excitement mixes with insecurity as she finger-combs her hair: *I didn't plan to go so short, but . . . I think it's cute? I hope? Gabriela will help me feel better—she's always honest.*

She feels a tap on her shoulder. "Gabriela!" Lisa fumbles the phone. "Sorry! Didn't see you."

"Too busy checking your teeth for coffee stains, I see," Gabriela teases, leaning in for a quick hug.

"Ha ha." Lisa steps back and waits, tucking a bit of hair behind one ear with a shy smile. Silence stretches between them.

Gabriela ducks her head, digging into her bag. "You ready to order?"

"Uh, yeah. Sure," Lisa stammers. *How could she not notice?*

"Ha! Found you." Gabriela pulls out her wallet with a triumphant flourish. Her gaze skates across Lisa and lands on the "Order Here" sign.

"Need. Coffee." Gabriela is already moving.

Lisa follows. "Is that a new jacket?" she asks her friend's back. "It's cute."

"Not new, but thanks!" Gabriela throws a smile over one shoulder—Lisa thinks it looks forced—and turns to place her order.

Lisa's heart plummets. *She definitely noticed that time. Her eyes totally paused.*

Gabriela is laughing with the barista, but Lisa hardly hears over the chaos of her own thoughts. *She hates it. She's just pretending she hasn't noticed so she doesn't hurt my feelings.* Disappointment, laced with hurt and anger, sours her stomach. *Ugh, I knew I shouldn't have gone with this cut.*

By the time they head to a table with their mugs, Lisa's insides are churning. *It's not just my hair—Gabriela's mad. I bet she's annoyed I didn't remember her jacket.* She slumps into the chair across from Gabriela and bursts out, "Don't lie—just tell me you hate it!"

Gabriela pauses with her steaming mug halfway to her lips. Her dark eyes go squinty. "My coffee? I haven't tasted it yet!"

"My hair," Lisa moans, flapping one hand toward the bob. "I *knew* I shouldn't have let Arturo talk me into cutting so much. Now it'll take months to grow out and I need to go into hiding and—"

"You cut your hair?" Gabriela stares at Lisa's head as if a nest of snakes had suddenly appeared there.

Now it's Lisa's turn to squint. "Wait, what? You seriously didn't notice?"

Gabriela shakes her head with a guilty laugh. "No, I'm so sorry."

A flush of mortification creeps up Lisa's neck; her ears blaze.

Gabriela studies Lisa's hair for several agonizing seconds before pronouncing, "It's adorable! I love it!" She takes a decisive sip of coffee.

"You're just saying that. And now I'm fishing for compliments." Lisa blows on her latte, wishing the mug were big enough to hide behind.

Gabriela makes a face. "Lisa, I am many things—including a horrible noticer of details, clearly—but I am not a giver of false compliments. I love it. I just honestly didn't notice because I was way too excited about getting coffee."

"Really?" Relief flows, warming her inside.

"Really."

Lisa allows herself a smile and takes a sip.[*]

\* \* \*

Sound familiar? I've been there myself too many times to count. If you're a big feeler, chances are you've had some version of this conversation approximately five million times. You've gotten carried away by unsubstantiated feelings that made you act weird toward someone you love. Made something out of nothing. Invented conflict. Read vibes into vibe-less situations.

Maybe you've felt insecure, worried that people disliked you or were talking behind your back. You saw coworkers or classmates or church friends huddled in a group, and you thought, *They're talking about me. And even if they aren't, they don't want to talk to me. I can't go over there.*

Maybe you've felt guilty and unworthy, convinced God was angry with you in some way, though you couldn't pinpoint a particular sin.

---

[*] Many thanks to Lisa, my too-cute-for-words-even-with-short-hair sister-in-law, for sharing this story.

## BUT IT FEELS SO REAL . . .

The trouble with big feelings is—well, a nice way of saying it is they are gifted. But like all superheroes, they possess a character flaw: sometimes they lie. Twist the truth. Exaggerate. Magnify minor details. Misinterpret situations and people. In their defense, the deception is often unintentional—our feelings are simply off-kilter and require recalibration.

And for the big feeler, who experiences so many powerful emotions, this leads to a complicated relationship with feelings. On the one hand, they are our constant, most intimate companions, so we trust them. We love them! They bring us joy and delight, affection and connection. But . . . *but*. There are the times when, like a mischievous friend, they lead us astray. They send us on emotional wild-goose chases, making us try to track down their sources—sources that may not even exist. They whirl us around till we can't tell ground from sky. They confuse and frustrate us—and we, in turn, may confuse and frustrate our friends and family.

If you are a steady feeler or a reluctant feeler, you are not immune to this struggle. Although you may not experience intense feelings as often as big feelers do, when big feelings knock at your door, they are still forceful. Convincing. Perhaps even *more* convincing for you than the big feeler—you don't get overpowered by emotions very often, so when you do, the emotion must be true . . . right?

Here's the thing: no matter what kind of feeler you are, intense emotions *always* feel real. And far be it from me to suggest that the feelings themselves are not real—we feel what we feel, and in that sense, our feelings are real. They are always real in the sense that they exist. But let's not equate the fact that we feel a certain feeling with that feeling itself representing a fact! (I know—that was a brain bender. Read it twice and you'll get it!) Because sometimes our feelings are just feelings, not truth. Let me say that again:

sometimes feelings are just feelings. Feelings are not facts. Just because we feel a thing does not make it true. For example:

- We may feel like a friend is mad at us . . . but our friend feels no such thing!
- We may feel like we're doing a terrible job at work . . . but our boss couldn't be happier with us.
- We may feel like God is out to get us because life is hard . . . but God adores us and wants to see us through hardship.

Feelings aren't the same thing as facts. And (as you well know) this inconsistency can get us into trouble. In families. In friendships. At church. At work. In faith. In prayer. In our struggle to accept forgiveness from God and from people. As we embark on this journey to living emotionally whole and healthy lives, I hope you'll fight to accept this key lesson: feelings don't necessarily equal truth. Do some feelings reflect truth and reality? Of course. But not all.

Let's take a look at someone in Scripture who, like us, had to learn the difference between feelings and facts. If you've never spent much time with Elijah, you're in for a kindred-spirit treat. Elijah, one of the most powerful Old Testament prophets, had an intensity to match his influence.

One of my favorite Elijah moments is recorded in 1 Kings 18–19. The word *moment* doesn't do it justice, as it's more an epic series of moments. First the miraculous and mighty: Elijah hosted a showdown with more than four hundred prophets of Baal atop a mountain. He called down fire from heaven, proving God's existence and supremacy. And then, after three long years of drought, Elijah asked God to make it rain. Sure enough, the heavens opened, and oh, how it rained.

At first, Elijah was flying high. But as adrenaline faded and holy fire turned to ash, Elijah thought: *What have I done? I just made a huge mistake.* The evil queen Jezebel agreed—she saw Elijah as a threat to her throne, and she put a bounty on his head. Elijah—calling-fire-and-rain-from-heaven Elijah, defeating-hundreds-of-enemies-in-one-day Elijah—ran for his life.

Elijah then went into a depressive episode that should give us all hope for our Pit of Despair days.

The story goes like this:

Elijah was afraid and ran for his life. . . . He came to a broom bush, sat down under it and prayed that he might die. "I have had enough, LORD," he said. "Take my life; I am no better than my ancestors." Then he lay down under the bush and fell asleep.

All at once an angel touched him and said, "Get up and eat." He looked around, and there by his head was some bread baked over hot coals, and a jar of water. He ate and drank and then lay down again.

The angel of the LORD came back a second time and touched him and said, "Get up and eat, for the journey is too much for you." So he got up and ate and drank. Strengthened by that food, he traveled forty days and forty nights until he reached Horeb, the mountain of God. There he went into a cave and spent the night.

1 KINGS 19:3, 4-9

Even though God had given Elijah an angel to care for him, plus more than forty days to rest and recover, the prophet was still in a rough place. Still hiding, still wishing he was done with this life, still asking God to end it all. (And here we all breathe a sigh of relief—even the greatest of prophets struggled with despair and darkness. And we're about to see what gentleness God showed him!)

But it was time for Elijah to pull out of the depths. Time for a talk with the Lord on a mountaintop. Time to face the facts. It went something like this:[*]

Wind writhes. Earth shakes.

The Lord is in neither wind nor earthquake, but he is coming.

Outside Elijah's cave, a fire flares, hot and reaching. Elijah shrinks back, pressing against the slick back wall, a babe in a womb. But the Lord is not in the fire. The fire dies, blown away by a soft breeze.

*The Lord.*

Elijah pulls his cloak over his face, hiding his eyes, and stumbles to the mouth of the cave on trembling legs.

A quiet voice calls, brushing silk-like against his ears. "What are you doing here, Elijah?"

Elijah starts to speak but comes up empty. He tries again; only a rasp comes out. "I have been very zealous for the Lord God Almighty." He clears his throat and picks up steam, words coming louder and faster: "The Israelites have rejected your covenant, torn down your altars, and put your prophets to death with the sword."

He finishes in a tumble of words, his voice high and tight: "I am the only one left, and now they are trying to kill me too." He stands panting, cringing, unsure if God will comfort him or kill him.

The Lord's voice is firm—intimidating, but not unkind. "Go back the way you came, and go to the Desert of Damascus. When you get there, anoint Hazael king over Aram. Also, anoint Jehu son of Nimshi

---

[*] The dialogue is drawn word for word from 1 Kings 19, NIV. The rest, as you may be growing accustomed to, is my own imagination filling in the blanks.

king over Israel, and anoint Elisha son of Shaphat from Abel Meholah to succeed you as prophet. . . . Yet I reserve seven thousand in Israel—all whose knees have not bowed down to Baal and whose mouths have not kissed him."

*   *   *

Let's take a closer look at this exchange. During Elijah's struggle with depression, our compassionate God sent an angel bearing comfort food (as my dad says, this was the original angel food cake!). He also gave the exhausted prophet forty days to rest. Then God invited Elijah to express his feelings, discouraging as they were. Isn't it reassuring that Elijah felt safe enough with God, confident enough in his patience and kindness, to verbalize his true feelings? This serves as a reminder to us that God always invites respectful honesty in our relationship with him.

The intense battle with the prophets of Baal left Elijah drained and lonely. The flight from Jezebel left him afraid and vulnerable. His feelings had taken over, and he couldn't think clearly, couldn't find his way out of the emotional pit.

What did God do for Elijah? First, he gave Elijah specific instructions, a mission. A reason to get out of the cave and back into life. (A purposeful to-do list is always helpful when pulling out of a season of sadness!) And then God gave Elijah the facts: "Yet I reserve seven thousand in Israel." Elijah *felt* alone, but in fact he was not alone—he was one of seven thousand who still served God. His feelings didn't represent the facts—far from it!

## SEPARATING FACT FROM FEELING

What can we learn from Elijah? When negative feelings get the best of us—particularly feelings of depression and discouragement, doom and defeat—the facts can be our friends. But with so many big feelings swirling inside him, Elijah wasn't able to see the facts himself. He needed another perspective—God's perspective.

When our feelings take over, when we are down and discouraged, let's seek truth. That leads us to our first skill in separating fact from feeling.

## Skill #1: Make your feelings face the facts.

We have to learn how to make our feelings face the facts—facts in general and facts from Scripture. You and I probably won't experience the same kind of face-to-face conversation with God that Elijah did, so how can we find God's voice? We can search his Word for truths that transcend time to touch our own lives. Whenever we feel intense emotions, we can train ourselves to stand those feelings up against Scripture to see how they line up.

Jesus gave us a great example of this skill when he spent forty days in the wilderness, fasting and preparing for his ministry. At the end of his fast, he was weak and hungry. In that moment Satan, sneaky snake, showed up to tempt him. And how did he tempt Jesus? He appealed to Jesus' feelings. First he spoke to the simple desire for food and physical comfort; next he tried to tap into the desire for approval, accolades, and power; and last he tried to incite insecurity in Jesus' relationship with God.

How did Jesus respond to each of Satan's temptations? With Scripture.

> The devil said to him, "If you are the Son of God, tell this stone to become bread."
>
> Jesus answered, "*It is written*: 'Man shall not live on bread alone.'"
>
> The devil led him up to a high place and showed him in an instant all the kingdoms of the world. And he said to him, "I will give you all their authority and splendor;

it has been given to me, and I can give it to anyone I want to. If you worship me, it will all be yours."

Jesus answered, "*It is written*: 'Worship the Lord your God and serve him only.'"

The devil led him to Jerusalem and had him stand on the highest point of the temple. "If you are the Son of God," he said, "throw yourself down from here. For it is written:

"'He will command his angels concerning you
    to guard you carefully;
they will lift you up in their hands,
    so that you will not strike your foot against a stone.'"

Jesus answered, "*It is said*: 'Do not put the Lord your God to the test.'"

When the devil had finished all this tempting, he left him until an opportune time.

LUKE 4:3-13 (EMPHASIS ADDED)

I encourage you to meet your feelings, as Jesus did, with facts from Scripture. When you feel godly emotions, bolster and expand those feelings with proof from Scripture. For example:

Feeling: I feel loved by God today.
Fact: I *am* loved by God today—and every day!
Scriptural proof: Psalm 147:11

Feeling: I feel different from the world. Isolated at work, alienated in class, an oddball online.
Fact: I *am* different from the world, and even though it can be difficult and lonely at times, being different is a good thing!
Scriptural proof: Hebrews 11:13-16

When your emotions do not reflect the truths of God, learn to contradict those feelings with Scripture:

Feeling: God's grace isn't big enough for me.
Fact: God is rich in grace, and he lavishes it on us generously.
Scriptural proof: Ephesians 1:3-8

Feeling: My little life doesn't matter to God.
Fact: God is big enough, wise enough, and loving enough
    to know what is going on with every individual on earth,
    and he cares about me.
Scriptural proof: Psalm 56:8-9

Let Scripture edit your feelings. It may not delete them, but it can clarify and revise them. Sometimes it might even rewrite them altogether.

Whatever you feel, let Scripture in. Let Genesis 9 send the rainbow into your flood. Let Psalm 103 send the Father's love into the fatherless place in your heart. Let Isaiah 40 send soaring wings to carry you through exhaustion. Let Jesus' voice give life to what has died in you.

## Skill #2: Distinguish feelings from facts.

We have a second important skill to develop: distinguishing feelings from facts. Because it's tough to meet your feelings with facts if you assume your feelings *are* the facts! So how do you tell the difference?

Big feelers often have a relentless commitment to honesty. We can't just dismiss a feeling, because it feels so real. Friends say, "Just let it go already, can't you?" All we can do is shake our heads and think, *If only it were that easy. I can't let it go in case it's true.* We have to get to the bottom of it. We have to find the truth. Only then can we move forward. Only then can we even consider letting it go.

So how exactly do we—big feelers, steady feelers, and reluctant feelers alike—determine whether a feeling represents truth? I like to break it down into three steps:

1. Acknowledge
2. Assess
3. Address or adiós

First, **acknowledge** what you're feeling. For example: *I feel like my friend is mad at me.*

When you have a heavy-weighted thought like this, it helps to drag it out of your secret thought world and thrust it into fresh air and sunlight. (Some toxic thoughts, like vampires, disintegrate the moment they hit sun.) You may even want to name your feeling out loud to another trusted friend—ideally a friend who knows you well and is spiritually mature enough that they won't run away screaming from some of your more out-there feelings. It also helps to write down your thoughts. Sometimes thoughts that sound oh-so convincing in our heads prove themselves imposters on paper.

Now **assess** whether the feeling represents truth. I find it helpful to ask myself a series of questions. This is where I put my feeling's integrity to the test. Why do I feel this way? What specific proof (if any) backs up this feeling? Again, I often do this on paper, because feelings can be notoriously slippery shape-changers; it's easier to nail down a feeling when you print it in black and white.

So in the *I-feel-like-my-friend-is-mad-at-me* example, I would assess it like this:

Why do I feel like she's mad at me?
*I feel distant.*

Remember, we're seeking facts, not feelings, so I push myself harder for details.

> *Why* do I feel distant? What specific events or interactions have made me feel that way?
> *Last night she didn't text me back; in fact, she's been slow responding to my messages for the past week. And this morning when a group of friends met for coffee, she didn't talk to me as much as usual. And when we* did *talk, she didn't ask how I'm feeling even though she knows I've been sick.*

> Have you and your friend had any conflict lately that you think she might be still upset about?
> *Not that I can think of, so . . . no.*

Now I need to either **address** or **adiós** the feeling (and of course by *adiós*, I mean we say goodbye to the feeling. We say goodbye in Spanish because we're fancy like that, though of course we are butchering Spanish grammar, because *adiós* is a salutation, not a verb). In the *is-my-friend-mad-at-me* example, since the feeling involves another person, I may need to have a conversation to figure out step three. In my case, I may need to ask my friend if something is bothering her.

If she says she *is* angry about something, then we need to address the conflict in our relationship. We need to talk it out, apologize where necessary, and offer forgiveness.[6]

If my friend says she isn't angry and everything is fine between us, then I need to take her at her word and release the feeling. She isn't mad at me. My feeling is simply untrue. Adiós, insecurity! I need to choose to let it go and think about other things.

Whether we address or adiós the feelings, they may not

immediately dissipate. I've found that, just as a bright light leaves a lingering neon glow against the back of your eyelids, so strong feelings can leave a residual outline that fades over time. But if you know the lights are just afterburn, it's easier to ignore them until they fade from memory altogether. You may still feel a little funky for a while, but less funky than before, and eventually not funky at all. (Remember the Twenty-Minute Rule!)

This ability to release is liberating and life changing, once you learn to do it. Once you workshop a feeling and decide that its season is over or it was never based in reality to begin with, I give you permission, by the authority vested in me by Walt Disney and by our mutual big feelings, to pull an Elsa and *let it go*.

Before we give our feelings license to run free in our hearts, affecting our mood and our relationships, let's stand them up beside the facts. When strong feelings clamor for our attention, let's take a moment to insist, "First the facts! Just the facts!" Only then will we be free to feel all the feels—the *real* feels.

## FEELING YOUR WAY FORWARD

### Prayer Prompt

I seek you with all my heart;
    do not let me stray from your commands.
I have hidden your word in my heart
    that I might not sin against you. . . .

I run in the path of your commands,
    for you have broadened my understanding.

Teach me, LORD, the way of your decrees,
    that I may follow it to the end.
Give me understanding, so that I may keep your law
    and obey it with all my heart.

Direct me in the path of your commands,
for there I find delight.

PSALM 119:10-11, 32-35

## Journal Prompts

1. Feelings hold different power over different people. Some of us are tangled up by insecurity; others are blinded by perceived injustice; others are tripped up by discouragement (and the list goes on). Which specific feelings make it most difficult for you to think clearly and find the facts?

2. Try the exercise described on page 90. List a specific feeling, then find a passage or two that either confirms or contradicts the feeling. Keep those Scriptures handy so you can easily reference them whenever you need a reminder of God's truths.

3. Try the exercise listed on page 92. Acknowledge a feeling you've been struggling with, then assess it using Scripture as a guide. If it's a valid feeling, address it as specifically as you can, both on paper and (if needed) in person, until you achieve some resolution. If your assessment reveals that the feeling is untrue, bid it a hearty "Adiós!"

# PART TWO

# WHAT SPECIFIC FEELINGS
# TEND TO TRIP US UP?

# CHAPTER 7

# ANXIETY:
# WHEN THOUGHTS GO BLENDER

I stumble out of the church building toward the car—a toddler on one hip, a grumpy five-year-old clawing at the other hip, and two other children waddling behind me like hangry ducklings. My overflowing diaper bag drops a Hansel-and-Gretel trail of Sunday school crafts onto the sidewalk behind us.

My preacher-husband catches up to me. "I'll-go-home-and-get-the-baby-down-for-a-nap," I huff, finally pausing for breath. "And then you can nap-watch golf while I get your Father's Day dinner started." I attempt an *it's-no-trouble-I'm-delighted-to-celebrate-your-wonderfulness* smile. Kevin, reading the stress in my voice (and all over my face and body) grabs our seven-year-old son by the hand. "I'm craving barbecue. I'll take Blake and we'll run through a drive-thru and be home in twenty minutes."

"Thanks," I breathe. This is one of those days when herding one fewer kid somehow feels like five hundred fewer.

Kevin claps Blake on the shoulder. "C'mon, son. Let's go get man food. Man cannot live on peanut butter and jelly alone. Especially not on Father's Day." He winks at the look of protest on my face.

"Hey! I make a mean PB and J. It's the after-church lunch of champions."

Kevin raises one eyebrow. "At our house, it's the every-day lunch of champions."

I give him the evil eye. "I would punch you if my arms weren't full of baby."

He laughs and swings Blake up onto his shoulder like a sack of flour, and they wrestle their way to the car, laughing.

Forty-five minutes later, the girls are finishing their PB and Js, and the baby is in bed. I glance at the clock. *Where are the boys? They should have been back twenty-five minutes ago.*

I call Kevin. No answer. I send a text: *Y'all coming home soon?*

I put the phone down and wipe peanut butter slime off little faces, certain I'll hear the *ding* of a reply soon. But there's no ding. The girls run giggling into the playroom, leaving a whiff of peanut butter in the air behind them.

"How many times do I have to remind that man to turn his ringer back on after church?" I mutter through my teeth, wiping the table with a little more force than necessary.

"Mommy! My sock is crooked and I can't get it straight!" The voice from the other room tips dangerously towards a wail.

"Shhh," I hiss-shout as soft-loud as I can. "You'll wake the baby!" I rush into the playroom to straighten the sock, then reenter the kitchen chuckling at this bizarre life I'm leading: Savior of the Socks. Provider of the Peanut Butter.

My eyes stray to the clock. The boys are now thirty minutes late.

I take a deep breath. *It's fine,* I tell myself. *Drive-thru lines can be murder on Sundays after church. Especially on Father's Day.*

But anxiety slithers into my gut. It's just a little worm sliding around, nibbling at my insides, but I feel unsettled. And annoyed. And dumb. But paranoia wins, and I pick up the phone and call Kevin again. No answer.

The worm morphs into a baby snake. I try to ignore it, yanking steaks out of the fridge and putting them in a pan to marinate.

Every thirteen seconds, I glance at my phone. After eight glances—they are now forty minutes late—I shove the steaks back into the fridge and wash my hands. I bang out another text: *Where are you guys? Getting worried.*

*It's fine,* I tell myself. *They probably just went inside to eat and Kevin's phone is still off. Don't freak out.*

I don't listen to myself.

Over the next twenty minutes, I call twice and text four times. My stomach is now filled with a nest of snakes—twenty or thirty of them, hissing and writhing. My imagination kicks into overdrive, treating me to high-definition images of every worst-case scenario imaginable: a car crash, mangled father-son bodies on the side of the road. A terrorist holding up the restaurant, my son's blue eyes bright with fear. Sudden-onset amnesia, and poor, confused Kevin driving our starving son halfway across the continent.

When I hit the amnesia scenario, I realize I need intervention. I call my sister, nearly hyperventilating. Thank God she picks up.

My words squeak high and warbly from a throat tight with unshed tears. "Alexandra. Kevin and Blake left for the drive-thru after church and now they're an hour late and I can't reach Kevin and I'm pretty sure they're both dead and I've lost my husband and son *on Father's Day* and I'm going to have to raise these three girls totally alone and we'll kill each other without any testosterone in the house and I have no idea how I'll support them by myself and I know I'm crazy please tell me I'm crazy."

To her eternal credit, my sister does not laugh. Her voice doesn't even sound like it's hiding a laugh. Instead of telling me to pull it together, she offers to pray.

"Dear God, you know that Elizabeth is very worried about Kevin and Blake," she says. "We pray you will watch over them and bring them home safely—"

I interject. "And God, please make Kevin turn on his stupid phone and call me!"

Now Alexandra does laugh, just a tiny one. "And yes, God, please make Kevin turn on his stupid phone and call Elizabeth, and—"

From the other room, I hear a banging door. Happy squeals of greeting. A booming baritone voice—Kevin's.

"Oh, thank God," I breathe. "They're home." Reluctantly, the snakes start to slither away, leaving a pulsating trail of adrenaline behind. I am left hollow, shaky.

"See?" Alexandra says. "How's that for an answered prayer?"

"I love you," I tell my sister, already sheepish. "Sorry I'm a total psycho."

"It's okay. You're cute when you're psycho," she says.

"Liar. But thank you."

On wobbly knees, I rush through the house to slam into Kevin, half-hugging him, half-hitting him. "Where have you been?" I choke into his chest. "I seriously thought you died. And took Blake out with you. *On Father's Day!*"

Kevin laughs, then tips my head back and sees tears glittering in my eyes. "Oh! You're serious." Guilt flickers across his face. "I'm sorry. We ate in the restaurant, and the line was long."

"You could have called." I punch him in the chest then. Harder than necessary. I mean, it may be Father's Day, but still. The man could have called.

* * *

Alas, the Father's Day Debacle is not the isolated incident I want it to be. If I had time, I could tell you about the incident with my next-door neighbors' front porch light, which was blinking in a bizarre rhythm, almost like . . . wait, was that Morse code? How do you spell *help* in Morse code? Were they being held hostage? Maybe they'd sent one of their genius daughters to flash the lights and call for help! Were Kevin and I their only hope of rescue? I *may* have actually sent my husband over to check on them.

They were eating dinner. Not being held hostage.

But I'm sure they were happy to know it was time to replace their light bulb.

## FEELING ON PURPOSE

It seems the big-feeling gene also comes with a few bonus materials: a wild-imagination gene, a worst-case-scenario gene, and a capacity for anxiety that can escalate from 0 to Nascar in .2 milliseconds.

My fellow feeler, you and I have no choice in this. If we want to live a life that is healthy, holy, and happy, we have to pay close attention to our thought life. We won't just accidentally overcome anxiety. We won't wake up one day having mastered dark feelings in our sleep. We won't automatically outgrow our emotional struggles the way children outgrow onesie pajamas and lovie blankets.

Growth takes focus, consistency, and prayer. Of course, growth takes work for everyone, sensitive and not-so-sensitive alike. However, it's fair to say that emotional growth may take more focus, consistency, and prayer for big feelers, who contend with a hefty load of intense emotions. (But don't forget the upside: since we experience the thrill of growth and joy so fully, the rewards of our efforts may be even *greater* for us than they are for others!)

Before we address specific strategies and Scriptures to help us with anxiety, let's step back and acknowledge that God gave us reasonable anxious feelings for a purpose. If we're driving at night and the roads are slick, our anxiety tells us to drive carefully, which is a good thing. In such situations, God uses anxiety to keep us safe. However, when anxiety balloons to wild-imagination and worst-case-scenario levels, we have some mental and emotional work to do.

Again let me say that not all struggles with anxiety can be adequately addressed without medical guidance and intervention, and I encourage you to seek such help if you are living with persistent and debilitating anxiety. Some of the people I love most in this world have benefitted from such care, and I am forever thankful for the relief and freedom they have experienced. My husband, who is usually easygoing and unflappable, suffers from a form of claustrophobia. He can preach sermons to thousands; he can calmly quarterback an offense in a roaring stadium while three-hundred-pound defenders bear down on him—but please don't put him in a crowded elevator. Elevators, traffic jams, airplanes, and other confining situations feel, for Kevin, like torture chambers. How grateful we have been for his doctor's care.

But over the years, Kevin and I have learned that even when you receive medical treatment for an anxiety disorder, you still have to work on how you think and how you manage stress. The truth is, we *all* have to work on managing stress. Medical treatment may alleviate symptoms and help to restore chemical balance, but even so, it won't eliminate all sources of anxiety from life. Stress will always be part of this fallen world.

Whether we're dealing with chronic anxiety or occasional anxiety, we all have to learn to manage anxious thoughts when they elbow their way into our lives. We all have to train our thoughts, feed our faith, and seek more peace. Even if your doctor is working to help you with your anxiety, you have your own work to do at home.

And *that's* the aspect of anxiety we're going to focus on in this chapter. I'm not going to dive any deeper into the "Do you have an anxiety disorder?" and "Should you take medicine or seek therapy?" questions, because that's not my area of expertise. But I am going to introduce you to some biblical principles and practical guidelines you can add to your toolbox as you seek to better equip yourself to handle anxiety.

## THE ANTIDOTE TO FEAR

First, let's take a look at the Bible's message about anxiety. Basically, it's this: *Don't be anxious. Trust God instead.*

I know. Maybe you just ground your teeth in frustration; maybe you even rolled your eyes. I'm with you. I understand how frustrating it can feel when a problem that plagues you doesn't seem to be taken seriously. It's not that the Bible doesn't take anxiety seriously (quite the opposite!). It's just that God's solution is—well, straightforward and simple. Simple to understand, at least, if not simple to implement.

Let's consider a few key passages—verses you may have read a thousand times:

> The Lord is near. Do not be anxious about anything, but in every situation, by prayer and petition, with thanksgiving, present your requests to God. And the peace of God, which transcends all understanding, will guard your hearts and your minds in Christ Jesus.
>
> PHILIPPIANS 4:5-7

Jesus said to his disciples: "Therefore I tell you, do not worry about your life, what you will eat; or about your body, what you will wear. For life is more than food, and the body more than clothes. Consider the ravens: They do not sow or reap, they have no storeroom or barn; yet God feeds them. And how much more valuable you are than birds! Who of you by worrying can add a single hour to your life? Since you cannot do this very little thing, why do you worry about the rest? . . . Do not be afraid, little flock, for your Father has been pleased to give you the kingdom."

LUKE 12:22-26, 32

The message of these Scriptures is profoundly simple, but you know what? At its core, anxiety is not that complicated. It's difficult to deal with, yes; overwhelming at times, yes. But complicated? No. And when I'm anxious, I don't want—nor can I handle—a complex solution; I want a simple, straightforward path to peace. One I can cling to even when my brain puts my thoughts into a blender. And that's exactly the kind of path Scripture offers.

When I'm anxious, my thoughts spin fast and wild, a tornado of worries that tangle, loop in on themselves, and then multiply. Within seconds, it feels like I'm worrying about eighteen things—though in truth I may only be worrying about one thing eighteen ways. When the tornado dissipates, it leaves behind wreckage in the form of a giant rubber band ball of thoughts, all wrapped around each other.

In those cyclone-brain moments, I need a strategy for clear thinking. For untangling the knot. For separating a clump of seemingly inextricable worries into distinct, manageable threads that can be addressed one by one.

Before I even attempt to resolve my anxious feelings, I start by writing down what I'm worried about. This is the first step in taking that giant rubber band ball and separating the different components. I do my best to specifically identify what my actual worries are.

Here's a classic example from my life as a preacher's wife:

So-and-so responds strangely in a text message. My thoughts go blender. Here's what I'm thinking:

1. I'm worried that so-and-so is angry with me.

2. I'm afraid that so-and-so won't listen if I try to work things out.

3. I'm afraid that so-and-so will think badly of me.

4. I'm afraid that if so-and-so and I have a conflict we can't resolve, so-and-so will gossip about me.

5. If so-and-so gossips about me, people might take sides.

6. If people take sides, it could split the church.

7. If the church splits, all our local church relationships will explode.

8. If the church splits, my husband will lose his job.

9. If my husband loses his job, we'll have to move.
    Alternate #9: If my husband loses his job and can't find a new one, we'll have to move in with my oh-so-gracious in-laws.
    Alternate alternate #9: If my husband loses his job and

can't find a job and my in-laws can't take us in, we'll end up homeless on the streets.

(As you may have noticed, most of my anxiety-related scenarios end in some combination of kidnapping, death, and homelessness.)

All because of an awkward text message.

The very act of writing down my thoughts is helpful—I'm usually able to toss out a few of the most irrational ones right away. Then I set to work either addressing or dismantling the thoughts that remain.

## AN ANXIETY INVENTORY

Once I've identified the various threads that are causing my anxiety, I ask myself a few questions. Again, they're pretty simple and straightforward, but I've found the simple route most helpful in moments when my emotions are buzzing.

1. Do you believe God is all-powerful?

    If the answer is yes, then you believe God is able to help resolve your situation. Nothing you face and nothing you ask is too big or too difficult for him. Take a look at what Scripture says about the God we serve:

From eternity to eternity I am God.
    No one can snatch anyone out of my hand.
    No one can undo what I have done.
ISAIAH 43:13, NLT

    We are in God's hand—his all-powerful, all-loving hand. Forever. And when he intervenes, no one can stop him.

2. Do you really believe God cares about your life—down to the details?

If the answer is yes, then a huge portion of your anxiety vanishes—mist burned away by morning sun. Not only is God *able* to help us, but he cares enough to *want to*. If your answer is no, then it's no wonder anxiety has crept in! It's terrifying to think you're alone in this world, battling cosmic, arbitrary forces of pain and misfortune all by yourself. No one to protect you, no one to defend you, no one to hear your cries of pain.

When my husband and I went through our long season of infertility, I questioned God's love for us. I still believed in God, and I thought he loved humans en masse—you know, Jesus died to save the whole world and all that—but I questioned whether the idea of God loving individual humans (translation: loving *me*) was just wishful thinking. Just a crutch Christians lean on to make them feel better.

Here are some of the Scriptures I leaned on during that time as I wrestled to choose fact over feelings:

I am feeble and utterly crushed;
    I groan in anguish of heart.
All my longings lie open before you, Lord;
    my sighing is not hidden from you. . . .
Come quickly to help me,
    my Lord and my Savior.
PSALM 38:8-9, 22

Record my misery;
    list my tears on your scroll—
    are they not in your record?
PSALM 56:8

What is the price of two sparrows—one copper coin? But not a single sparrow can fall to the ground without your Father knowing it. And the very hairs on your head are all numbered. So don't be afraid; you are more valuable to God than a whole flock of sparrows.

MATTHEW 10:29-31, NLT

Cast all your anxiety on him because he cares for you.

1 PETER 5:7

These Scriptures prove that God loves me and you—not just plural you, *singular* you. He cares about your longing and sighing; he counts your hairs and knows your days. If you care about it, he cares about it. If you worry about it, he wants to know. If you hurt over it, he hurts alongside you. He counts your tears and holds them in his hand.

3. Do you believe God is kind enough to engage with your problems when you pray about them?

   If you believe God is kind enough not just to care about but also to involve himself in your daily life, your experience of life and hardship is transformed. The Bible doesn't promise that God will always swoop in Superman style to save the day and alleviate all your suffering, but it does promise that he will engage emotionally and help you through hard times. Even when he doesn't take away your problems, he is quietly at work: softening the pain, providing you with the encouragement and the people you need to make it through.

4. When your anxiety stems from conflict with another person, do you believe the Holy Spirit is able to help you find unity?

If you've experienced brokenness in your family life, you may have fears that people will fail or betray you in some way. As a preacher's wife, I tend to have a lot of ministry- and church-related fears: Will conflict destroy what we've worked so hard to build? Will sin come in and break us apart?

One of Jesus' primary desires is for unity—what a comfort to realize he wants it even more than we do! The night of his arrest, he prayed, "Holy Father, protect them by the power of your name, the name you gave me, so that they may be one as we are one" (John 17:11). Paul echoed this sentiment when he wrote to his fellow believers in Philippi, "Make my joy complete by being like-minded, having the same love, being one in spirit and of one mind" (Philippians 2:2).

When I feel anxious about relationships, particularly relationships with other believers, I am learning to call upon the Holy Spirit: "I know that you live in me—and in this other person. Please work on both of us to bring us together and heal whatever divides us. I trust that you want unity even more than I do, and you want to help us forge it."

## PUTTING THE BRAKES ON ANXIETY

Let's get even more practical. When anxious thoughts start flying, we have one of three choices: we can feed the fire, we can remain passive, or we can interrupt the cycle.

### 1. Feed the fire.

When you feed the fire, you think more anxious thoughts. Reinforce them by repeating them to yourself and adding new, higher stakes to the thoughts. Talk to reactive people who will help you tunnel into an even deeper rabbit hole. Read and watch things that confirm and expand your darkest fears. (WebMD, anyone? Within two minutes you'll diagnose a simple headache as a brain tumor, an aneurysm, or gangrene—or possibly all three.)

## 2. Remain passive.

When you remain passive, you don't actively feed the anxiety, but you aren't intentional about resisting it either . . . which basically ensures that the thoughts will take you wherever they want you to go (which is usually a very un-fun place involving panic and misery).

## 3. Interrupt the cycle of anxious thoughts.

The third option, interrupting the cycle, is the only one that allows us relief. The relief may not be perfect, and it may not be immediate, but most of the time we can at least stop things from getting worse. Equipped with Scripture and empowered by the Spirit, we can arrest the escalation. We can keep the tornado at an F1 instead of an F5.

But to do that, we have to stop whirling around the house, dervish-style, and slow down to work on our thoughts. As Paul encourages us to "work out [our] salvation with fear and trembling" (Philippians 2:12), so I urge you to work out your anxiety.

Here are a few practical steps to try as you train yourself to interrupt the cycle:

1. **Write your thoughts down.** Be as specific as you can, and number your thoughts one by one. This helps you to identify exactly what you are worried about. As I noted earlier, you sometimes find that you aren't worried about eighteen things; you are worried about one thing eighteen ways.

2. **Speak your fears out loud.** Expose your thoughts to open air. Fears that sound perfectly rational in your head—likely, even—may sound . . . well, if not ridiculous, at least *creative* when spoken aloud. I find it especially helpful to share my anxious thoughts with a trusted friend (*trusted* meaning "someone who won't laugh too hard at me or threaten me with a straitjacket"). My friend Emma and I take turns sharing wild anxieties with each other, everything from "I'm headed to the poorhouse," to "Is this bump on my neck a tumor?" to "My kid might need an exorcism." We don't just share—we talk each other off the ledge and back to a more realistic interpretation of our difficulties.

3. **Turn "what if" into "even if."** This might sound counterintuitive, but in some circumstances, it's actually helpful to take your anxious thoughts and play them out.[7] If you can't stop thinking, *What if . . . ?* just go with it. So let's say your current anxiety is *What if I can't finish my project on time and I have to turn it in late and my boss gets mad?*

Okay, let's play it out:

Best-case scenario: Your boss is running behind on the project anyway and doesn't care. You get a pass.

Worst-case scenario: You have an unforgiving boss or a history of chronic lateness at work, and you get fired. That's no fun, but if that happens, you pick yourself up and start praying and looking for another job. Eventually, you find a new job. Not fun, but totally survivable.

Medium-case scenario (Is that a thing? We're making it a thing): You turn your project in late. You talk to your boss, apologize, explain, and do your best to come up with a solution. You have a history of being a responsible employee and you have some "love in the bank" at work, so your boss says, "Don't let it happen again," and everyone moves on. Your boss and coworkers discover that you are an imperfect human just like they are. As an added bonus, you now have a great "I've been there" story to tell your kids when they freak out about turning their homework in late.

I've found this strategy productive when my imagination tries to hitch a ride on the what-if train. It engages the creative problem-solving part of my brain and helps me turn "*What if* this happens?" into "I'll be okay *even if* this happens."

My only caveat? Do not play out what-if scenarios involving death or kidnapping. It's not a helpful exercise. I speak from unfortunate experience.

All kidding aside, as Christians, we have the added encouragement of being able to put our trust in God. The confidence that even if the worst happens, we are not alone. We have God—and more important, God has us. There is no crisis, no misfortune, no heartache he cannot see us through. Even if our world is falling apart, God remains: the steady path beneath our stumbling feet, the comforting guide through the valley of shadows, the quiet water and sunlit pasture on the other side.

4. **Capture and reframe thoughts that include "I can't" and "I could never."**

  *I can't survive without this job.*
  *I can't endure a breakup.*
  *I could never keep my faith strong through a chronic illness.*

  When we say, "I can't" and "I could never," we hamstring ourselves and limit God. We pre-decide to fail, surrendering before a single thing has even happened! Not only that, but we underestimate our own resilience, discount the power of the Holy Spirit, and overlook the never-ending grace of God.

A healthier, more faithful way of thinking would be:

*I hope I don't have to survive without this job. But even if I do, God, the great Provider, can see me through.*

*I hope I don't have to endure a breakup. But even if I do, God is faithful and his love never fails.*

*I hope I don't get diagnosed with a chronic illness. But even if I do, God will provide the strength and resources—medical and financial and relational—that I need to make it through.*

\* \* \*

God takes our anxiety seriously. If we care about it, he cares about it too. But to him, the scenario we fear is not as terrifying or potentially world ending as it feels to us. He sees the big picture we cannot see. He knows how the story ends. He knows what he can do—and what he will do. Our God delights in surprise endings and eleventh-hour miracles. And even when he doesn't bail us out at the eleventh hour, even when the worst happens and things shatter, he is always there to draw us near—into his loving arms, into his lap—and knit us back together: "The LORD is close to the brokenhearted and saves those who are crushed in spirit" (Psalm 34:18).

Remember the passage we read in the beginning—Luke 12, Jesus' famous "Do not worry" message? Let's take another peek at it: "Since you cannot do this very little thing, why do you worry about the rest? . . . Do not be afraid, little flock, for your Father has been pleased to give you the kingdom." Did you catch that sweet term of endearment: *little flock*? I can picture Jesus looking protectively over his beloved followers as they sat listening—this one stressed about a difficult pregnancy, that one worried she'll never get married, this one agonizing over a wayward child, that one afraid arthritis will keep him from working to support his family—and loving each one with the fierce affection that filled his fiery breast. Affection so fierce it soon caused him to die to save them all. *Don't worry, little flock. I am good, and you are mine.* That is his same message to you and me even now.

When loved ones run late or loved ones run off, when thoughts run wild or life runs amok . . . you are in God's hand, and there you will stay.

## FEELING YOUR WAY FORWARD

**Prayer Prompt**

> The LORD makes firm the steps
>     of the one who delights in him;
> though he may stumble, he will not fall,
>     for the LORD upholds him with his hand.
>
> I was young and now I am old,
>     yet I have never seen the righteous forsaken
>     or their children begging bread. . . .
>
> For the LORD loves the just
>     and will not forsake his faithful ones.
>
> PSALM 37:23-25, 28

## Journal Prompts

1. List a few reasons why you believe God cares about your life—down to the details. Think of specific times when God has taken care of you or comforted you, and describe them.

2. When you think about the devotion and care God has already shown you, how does that change the way you view your current problems? How does it affect any worries you may be carrying?

3. Write down a "what if" scenario that makes you anxious. Now counter that fear by writing down some "even if" statements that help you view it differently.

# CHAPTER 8

# BORROWING BURDENS: WHAT'S YOURS IS MINE

The text feels wrong, though the words are innocuous enough: "I'll call you later."

Why would she need to *call* me to tell me about her ultrasound? Only last week she'd heard the baby's heartbeat for the first time, and there'd been no call—she'd just texted a thousand hearts and exclamation points.

I wait, heart in throat, life on hold, for her call. Her voice when I answer is dead. Dead as the precious little peanut inside, the babe we have fasted and wept and pleaded for these three long years, both of us infertile together.

A month earlier—glory!—we'd both gotten pregnant in the same two-week window. It had been a gift beyond hoping, better than any fantasy scenario we could have concocted in our most feverish prayers.

For a few short weeks, all had been right with the world. God was good—so very good. For him to grant both our prayers at the same time, allowing us to escape the anguish of infertility together, pregnant with miracle babies due within two weeks of each other—it was a dream.

And indeed it had been a dream. Just a dream.

And now in the crack of my friend's voice I hear the fragile fantasy shatter, the glass shards dangerous on the floor. Already it's cut her a thousand ways; I hear it in the way her pitch goes flat—no rise, no fall, as if echoing the lifeless heart within. "I need surgery," she says. "Tomorrow."

"Oh, friend," I say. "I'll pray."

We hang up. Long minutes I hold the phone in a limp hand. Guilt tortures me. As my friend makes awful phone calls and preps for surgery, inside me a tiny heart still flutters, a blessed baby still grows.

"I can't," I cry to my husband, my eyes tear-blind, my throat raw. "I can't be pregnant without her. How can I sit here and celebrate my baby while she's losing hers? I can't . . . I can't even be happy about our baby anymore."

Kevin grabs both of my hands and waits till I drag my eyes up to meet his. His voice is gentle. "Elizabeth, this situation is heartbreaking, and of course we will be sad with them. But you can't mourn in her place. You can't take on her loss as if it were your own. We begged God for our baby, and as sad as we are for our friends, it would dishonor him if we didn't continue to thank him and celebrate."

I bow my head, wrestling with the guilt that insists, *How dare you be happy?* But finally I give a nod. Because Kevin is right. Even if I lock joy out of my own heart, it won't diminish my friend's grief.

\*　\*　\*

We big feelers are the emotional Sherpas of the world, inviting friends and family to pile their worries and fears on our empathetic shoulders. Heartache and hurt call to us. "No one should carry their burden alone," we say. "Let me carry that with you—or better yet, for you." This is often such an instinctive response that we don't even realize we're doing it. And we don't just do this for friends and family; these wide-open hearts of ours also have a tendency to take on the sorrows of strangers—indeed, the world.

I've done it more times than I can count.

His name was Hunter. He was two and he loved Batman, just like my son did at that age. He was two and he never got to turn three. He died when a driver, high on heroin, rear-ended his mother's car early one weekday morning outside the Starbucks two miles from my house. It was a day for playing in parks, not dying in cars. The sun smiled when it should have draped itself in clouds; blue skies sang when they should have wept rain. I've often wondered, *Was Hunter's mother driving home from elementary school drop-off with her toddler in the back seat, just like I was that morning? Why Hunter and not my Sawyer? Why Hunter's family and not ours?*

It's been five years—five years when Hunter should have gone to kindergarten, lost teeth, learned to whistle, laughed ten thousand times—but instead of celebrating those milestones, his family adds to his shrine at the busy street corner where he died: ribbons, teddy bears, toys. They don't know me, but I pray for them. Remember with them. Mourn with them.

I could tell you a hundred more stories like these—melancholy ghosts that haunt me. But I don't need to, do I? Because you have your own burdens you've borrowed: Strangers' sorrows. Friends' griefs. Loved ones' pain. (And now I feel guilty for adding more stories to your pile of grief—sorry.)

So what do we do about this, my fellow softhearted friends? How do we live with these tender hearts of ours without either imploding from pain or shutting off and shutting down? How do we make it through the daily onslaught of sad stories, the lifelong parade of hurting souls? How do we walk around without dangling on the edge of despair? How do we not live huddled in the corner, ears plugged, shouting, "La-la-la-I'm-not-listening"?

You might expect the message of this chapter on borrowing burdens to be, "Grow thicker skin. Stop letting everyone else's burdens affect you."

It's not.

If you could grow thicker skin, you would have done so by now. And even if you *did* manage the unlikely feat of growing thicker skin—a process that I believe would require hardening and perhaps scarring your heart—then you would cease to be you. Empathetic, exquisitely emotional you—the precious soul God so painstakingly and purposefully designed in your mother's womb.

We're going to talk about ways—first biblical, then practical— to better manage other people's feelings when they cross our boundaries, enter our hearts, and affect our internal environment. Our aim is to identify Christlike practices and thought patterns that will empower us to come out of hiding and venture into the wild world with our hearts open, the way we were meant to live.

## BORROWING BURDENS VERSUS SHARING THEM

There's a significant difference between borrowing people's burdens and sharing them. *Borrowing* a burden means we attempt to take a load off someone's shoulders and place it on our own. We say, "Hey, I know this is yours, but can I take it home with me?" We act as if the loss, the responsibility, the breakup, the debt, the struggle were our very own. Borrowing burdens is our attempt to stand in someone else's place when they are suffering, to take over their pain. And noble as that desire may be, none of us can suffer in another's place. Only Jesus can do that—and he has already done it.

You and I can hurt *with* people, but not *for* them. No matter how hard we hurt, we won't be able to take their pain away.

But *sharing* a burden means the other person carries their load and we take a bit of the weight off. We may share their load by feeling some of their pain and offering sympathy, perhaps offering emotional and practical support. We may grab hold of a corner of their box of pain and help them lug it up the stairs; we might even stick around and help them unpack. But when we leave, we don't take the entire box home to keep forever.

Eight years after my friend lost her baby, I found myself on the other end of the phone call: the one with the broken voice and lifeless womb. No one could mourn for me, no one could take away even one tear—but they could feed my family while I recovered from surgery. No one could abbreviate my journey through grief, but they could push past the awkward and ask, "How are you feeling?" even if they weren't sure it was okay to ask. They could listen while I processed the ache, the loss, the *why*. And in those sacred shared moments, the pain was lighter; the hope of healing burned brighter. No, my friends and family couldn't shorten the painful part of my path, but they made it less lonely. And in their hot meals and listening ears and kind words I felt the hands—and heart—of God. Reaching out and loving me. Drawing me close so I'd know he hadn't left me alone in the valley.

Let's not underestimate the power of sharing burdens with loved ones for a time. Small acts of kindness, thoughtful words, earnest prayers—when we offer these gifts, we acknowledge and validate their pain, and that, too, is a gift.

A brief word to reluctant feelers, who may be a bit overwhelmed with all this talk about feeling others' pain. You may be thinking, *I don't even want to feel my own pain—now I'm supposed to feel others' pain, too?*

Your struggle may be just the opposite of the big feeler's. You may not be tempted to borrow others' burdens; you might prefer to keep their pain at arm's length. Sharing pain is uncomfortable, intimate, and—well, painful. But Paul urges us not to shut our hearts against others' hurts: "Rejoice with those who rejoice; mourn with those who mourn" (Romans 12:15); "Share each other's burdens, and in this way obey the law of Christ" (Galatians 6:2, NLT). Remember that God is not asking you to shoulder others' burdens in their stead, but he does call us all to offer compassion, kindness, and (this may be your favorite part!) practical care.

As a reluctant feeler, you may feel most comfortable when your contribution falls less under the "dump all your feelings on me and I'll offer an empathetic listening ear" category and more under the "acts of service" domain. Hands-on service is an invaluable way to comfort hurting hearts; in fact, Jesus gave us this great promise: "If anyone gives even a cup of cold water to one of these little ones who is my disciple, truly I tell you, that person will certainly not lose their reward" (Matthew 10:42). God sees and values our acts of service; through our hands and our gifts, he reaches out to comfort his children in need. So share others' burdens in whatever way you can, using the gifts God has entrusted to you, so that you, in turn, might give.

## BEARING BURDENS, JESUS STYLE

Of the many things I appreciate about Jesus, one is the example he left behind: he didn't just tell us what to do; he *showed us how.* Of course, Jesus is different from us in many ways, especially this: Jesus *did* take on the entire burden of the world's sins, bearing it all on his sinless shoulders—and none of us can imitate that sacrifice.

It was made once for all, and we can only accept it with gratitude and devotion.

With the understanding that we will reflect Jesus imperfectly and incompletely, let's take a look at how Jesus conducted his daily life—specifically, how he related to hurting people.

## Man of Sorrows

You think *you* attract heartache and hurt? Isaiah prophesied that Jesus would be "a man of sorrows, acquainted with deepest grief" (Isaiah 53:3, NLT). Jesus was the ultimate pain magnet—not only because his compassion drew hurting people to him, but because he alone could actually *do something* about people's pain. The sick and hurting flocked to him (*stampeded* might be a more accurate word) till he almost had to become a recluse. Wherever he was, whole towns gathered. Houses overflowed. The Twelve had to commandeer boats so Jesus could preach without being trampled. Even when Jesus tried to retreat, crowds chased him across lakes and showed up hungry (and of course he fed them).

And how did Jesus respond to this constant flood of human suffering?

Jesus let people's pain in. He let *people* in. "He took up our pain and bore our suffering," Isaiah tells us (verse 4). We hear it in the words he cried out as he entered the city that would soon nail him to a cross: "Jerusalem, Jerusalem, you who kill the prophets and stone those sent to you, how often I have longed to gather your children together, as a hen gathers her chicks under her wings, and you were not willing" (Luke 13:34).

Like some of us, Jesus could be a sympathy crier. In John 11, he stood outside his friend Lazarus's tomb alongside his sisters. Even though Jesus knew he was about to call Lazarus out of death, back to life, he was apparently so overcome by the sisters' grief that he wept with them (see John 11:1-44).

Jesus loved people in some of the same ways big feelers do: quickly, intensely, publicly. Take a look at these two interactions:

> Jesus went to a town called Nain, and his disciples and a large crowd went along with him. As he approached the town gate, a dead person was being carried out—the only son of his mother, and she was a widow. And a large crowd from the town was with her. *When the Lord saw her, his heart went out to her* and he said, "Don't cry."
> LUKE 7:11-13 (EMPHASIS ADDED)

The Greek word translated "his heart went out to her" (*splagch-nizomai*) is a visceral word meaning "his insides went out" to her (the Greeks viewed the intestines as the seat of our emotions). Now *that's* a deep feeling!

Here's another encounter:

> As Jesus started on his way, a man ran up to him and fell on his knees before him. "Good teacher," he asked, "what must I do to inherit eternal life?" . . .
> *Jesus looked at him and loved him.* "One thing you lack," he said. "Go, sell everything you have and give to the poor, and you will have treasure in heaven. Then come, follow me."
> At this the man's face fell. He went away sad, because he had great wealth.
> MARK 10:17, 21-22 (EMPHASIS ADDED)

How exactly did observers notice Jesus' love for these two people? Did his eyes well up with empathetic tears for the heartbroken mother? When he met the rich young ruler, did he offer an eye-crinkling smile? A shoulder pat of greeting? We don't know those details, but we do know what Jesus did *after* he met these people—and his words and actions can instruct us in our habit of borrowing burdens.

In the first story, Jesus was so moved that he halted the funeral procession by touching the coffin (see Luke 7:14), a shocking breach of convention that made Jesus ceremonially unclean. With the whole procession surely gaping, Jesus woke the young man from the dead and gave him back to his mother. What a tender reunion that must have been! We don't know how long Jesus stayed to minister in the town of Nain, but we know it couldn't have been long, because he kept traveling from town to town, preaching and healing (see Luke 8:1).

In the second story, Jesus looked at a man, loved him . . . and then called him to sell everything and follow him. Hope drained from the man's face. He shuffled away sad, unwilling to accept this cost. Did Jesus chase after this promising young man? Did he shout, "Wait!" and then grab him by the arm, pulling him aside for a heart-to-heart? Did he appeal to him, describing the treasure that awaits in heaven—a treasure far greater than any earthly riches the man might give up? No. Jesus let this man—this man he loved—walk away. Naturally, the disciples were "amazed at his words" (Mark 10:24)—left scratching their heads and raising their eyebrows, as people so often were around Jesus.

So what can we learn from our Lord's example? His heart went out to people; he loved instantly and intensely—but even so, he didn't hang around trying to fix everything for everyone he loved. In fact, Jesus didn't even heal every sick person he encountered. Take a look at John 5, where Jesus went to a place filled with "a great number of disabled people," and he only healed one. One! And then (most likely trying to avoid pandemonium) Jesus slipped through the crowd before the man could even figure out who had healed him.

Some of the reasons for his actions were practical. Even Jesus was confined to twenty-four-hour days. Even Jesus was limited by a human body that required food and sleep. Even Jesus didn't have time in his short three-year ministry to physically heal everyone.

Here are a few lessons we can learn about burden bearing from Jesus' interactions with those in need of help:

1. Jesus was more concerned with people's spiritual well-being than their physical well-being.

   He didn't consider earthly afflictions to be the most heartbreaking thing that could happen to a person—in fact, when he later crossed paths with the man he'd healed by the pool, Jesus said to him, "Stop sinning or something worse may happen to you" (John 5:14). Jesus knew that spiritual death was a fate far worse than physical paralysis.

2. Jesus knew that he would soon offer a path to ultimate healing—of body *and* soul—for everyone.

   Perhaps the knowledge of his impending crucifixion and resurrection allowed Jesus to keep moving when time (or other limitations) didn't permit him to heal every sick person or meet every need.

3. Jesus accepted his limits.

   In coming to earth as a human, Jesus accepted the limitations of earthbound life: Only so much time in each day. Only so far his feet could walk. Only so many people his hands could touch. Although he loved everyone, he could not personally serve and heal everyone, so he loved and served and healed those he could, and he devoted his life to equipping others, who would one day equip and serve others, who would one day equip and serve still others. And in that way, he knew that his love and healing would know no limits.

4. Jesus embraced his ultimate goal: the Cross.

Although Jesus was a powerful speaker, his ultimate goal was not preaching. Although Jesus was a great healer, his ultimate goal was not healing. Although Jesus could transform single-serve snacks into feasts for thousands, his ultimate goal was not eliminating hunger. Although Jesus cared for the lonely and despised, his ultimate goal was not social justice. Jesus' ultimate goal was the Cross: "I have a baptism to undergo," he said, "and what constraint I am under until it is completed!" (Luke 12:50). With dogged focus and determined courage, he marched on toward Calvary, to the sacrificial death that now saves us all.

5. Jesus let people make up their own minds.

When it came to spiritual issues such as sin and salvation, Jesus called people to change, but he knew they had to decide for themselves. He didn't hang around trying to coax them into it. He presented the cost and the call, then left the decision up to them.

## Sovereign God

Jesus maintained a big-picture perspective, a long view on life.

My natural unconscious assumption is this: *Evil and suffering deserve to be mourned fully, but they also need to be alleviated as quickly as possible.* And honestly, I fight suffering—as in, jaw-grinding, fist-shaking, shout-praying fight it.

Part of the reason we feel so devastated by losses—our own and those of others—is because our limited human vision, trapped in this one dimension we can see, can't fathom the spiritual realm or the end game. We don't appreciate the long view.

We don't see how a particular kind of suffering may be an integral way God is shaping a person into who he wants them to be. (I'm not suggesting that the suffering is the person's fault, only that God may have purposes for the suffering.) Pastor and writer Timothy Keller puts it this way: "One of the main teachings of the Bible is that almost no one grows into greatness or finds God without suffering, without pain coming into our lives like smelling salts to wake us up to all sorts of facts about life and our own hearts to which we were blind."[8]

We don't see how God is able to pull a Romans 8:28 on our suffering—to bring something good from even the greatest of losses. I'm not saying the suffering itself is good (in the sense of being a positive experience or a source of joy), but the growth and depth and faith that can emerge in the end can be good. Those good things do not replace the loss, but perhaps they redeem it to some degree, giving it spiritual meaning.[9]

When we embrace this perspective on suffering—when we bring God into the way we view suffering—we are less likely to mourn in an unhealthy way with people, as if both our worlds were ending. We are better able to show compassion and offer words and actions of comfort without also feeling pressure to solve the problem ourselves. We are better able to release the burden into God's capable hands, knowing he is acting and intervening and comforting and helping where he sees fit. Working even when and where we can't see.

## TYPES OF BURDEN BORROWERS

Let's get a bit more practical. Because truth? We may know in our heads that we shouldn't take on other people's hurts, but sometimes our soft hearts seem to have minds of their own. No matter what we tell our hearts to do, if someone else's pain comes knocking, our hearts tend to fling open the door and make up the guest bed.

If you're like me, you've tried to lock other people's pain out a million times. But telling yourself to stop caring about and feeling for others is like telling yourself to stop breathing. Maybe you can hold your breath for a minute or so, but eventually your body will force you to take a breath. My rather unorthodox advice is this: stop trying to close off your heart. Stop trying to stop hurting for other people. If you hear about someone who's hurting and the hurt comes in and hurts you, too—let it on in.

I know. I told you this advice was unorthodox. But let's cede to reality: if you try to lock others' pain out, you'll only be fighting a losing battle. You might manage to ignore the knock at the door for a while, but eventually you won't be able to stand it. Then you'll end up opening the door while feeling sad for the hurting person *and* frustrated with yourself, perhaps even guilty. So how can we offer empathy without going to extremes? Feel sympathy without suffocating under the weight of it?

I have some practical steps to share, but first let's figure out what kind of burden borrower you are. We all borrow burdens, but we do so in different ways. Although the following list is not exhaustive, perhaps you will find yourself somewhere in it. (Or if you're like me, perhaps you'll find yourself in multiple descriptions . . . *sigh*.)

The Listener: This person says things like, "Knock, call, text, or carrier-pigeon me anytime, day or night. I will always be there, always listen. I may not be able to give advice or fix your problem, but please, dump your every feeling into my all-absorbing ears. I can take it." (Meanwhile, the

Listener cannot actually take it. The Listener struggles to sleep, eat, and remember their own name. The Listener's other relationships suffer. The Listener feels drained, exhausted, and occasionally resentful with a side order of guilt and self-loathing.)

**The Weeper:** A close relative of the Listener, the Weeper listens *and* weeps alongside hurting souls. They take "walking in their shoes" to a whole new deep-down-in-the-soul-not-to-mention-the-tear-ducts level. When a friend bleeds, the Weeper also needs a transfusion.

**The Fixer:** Not only does the Fixer listen, they are determined to *fix it*, doggone it! The Fixer researches and ponders, prays and plans. Gives advice. Offers support, food, housing, money. Checks in. Seeks updates. Wrings hands. Follows up. Rewrites the plan. Prods and nudges. Hand-holds. Never. Lets. Go.

**The It's-Somehow-My-Fault-er:** This sensitive soul suffers from a kind of survivor's guilt that makes them feel overly responsible for others' sufferings. They are plagued by thoughts like, *Why them and not me? They are more righteous/responsible/health conscious/fill-in-the-blank than I am—so why are they suffering instead of me? Maybe if I suffer with them, I can somehow alleviate the injustice—or better yet, show God how unfair this is.*

**The Down-in-the-Ditch-Together-Forever Borrower:** This person says, "If you fall into a ditch, I'm jumping down there with you every time." This kind of hard-core devotion is sometimes admirable, but it may get us into trouble when a loved one enjoys making ditches their permanent home.

**The I-Won't-Be-Happy-Till-You're-Happy Borrower:**
This burden borrower makes an internal vow, perhaps unconsciously, forbidding themselves from being happy until their friend/boyfriend/spouse/parent/child/whoever is happy. Their sufferings and joys are inextricably intertwined. And heaven help this poor sensitive soul when they make this pact with *every person they love.* If every person they love must be happy all at the same time in order for them to be happy, you can imagine (perhaps from personal experience) how often this person allows themselves to be happy.

Of course, it's not wrong to listen, weep, advise, share burdens, and even jump in the ditch to comfort hurting loved ones. But we have to guard against extremes that damage our own hearts and end up limiting our ability to live life—which in turn limits our ability to help and comfort.

When you're tempted to try to take on someone else's suffering as your own, remember these practical truths:

1. Sitting around feeling depressed for and with someone else for a long period of time does not actually change their situation. It just paralyzes you, which prevents you from supporting them the way you want to. It also keeps you from living your daily life.

2. It's one thing to borrow someone's burdens for a short time; it's another thing to keep renewing the loan. Sometimes it helps if we give ourselves time limits, like this: *I'm probably going to be sad alongside my loved one*

133

*for a few hours . . . or a few days, or even a season of days. But by X time, I need to surrender this in prayer. I will keep loving and supporting my friend, but I will deliberately take charge of my emotions so they don't linger in the depths for an unhealthy period of time.* (More on this to come later in the chapter.)

Remember: Giving in to long-term downward spirals can hurt the people closest to us. I don't say that to make us feel guilty when we struggle with depression, only to remind us not to deliberately indulge in negativity when we know we could choose another emotional path.

3. If someone you don't know well is suffering alone and you're tempted to take their suffering deep down into your heart, to carry it as your own, remember that there *is* someone who cares and carries the burdens of every person on earth: God. We can help others find strength in God without trying to take on God's responsibility for him (see 1 Samuel 23:16). He's already doing a great job.

## DEALING WITH THIN SKIN

Strange as it may sound, our cells have a lot to teach us about dealing with feelings. I still remember the day my seventh-grade chemistry teacher told me that I—along with twenty-nine other preteens suffering through *all kinds* of chemistry together in that hormone-rife cinder block classroom—was made up of trillions of invisible cells, I honestly didn't believe her. Even now, if I think about it too hard, the room tips sideways.

Every cell in the human body is surrounded by what I, in my nontechnical jargon, think of as a "skin"—a membrane, or outer wall. These membranes are semipermeable, meaning they allow some things to enter even as they keep others out. When external bodies pass through a cell's membrane and enter the cell, the cell has a decision to make: *Do I take this material and use it, or do I reject it and send it on its way?* The decision depends on the material. If the cell needs the material, it wraps it up in a special membrane and "eats" or "drinks" it. (I know—my scientific vocabulary is astounding, is it not?) In other words, the cell puts it to use—feeds off its power. However, if the cell identifies the material as either toxic or simply not useful, the cell rejects it and then ejects it.

We big feelers—with our thin, easily permeable emotional boundaries—can learn some important lessons from our cells. Every emotion that crosses the membrane into our hearts must be dealt with in some way. Just as the cell draws in the materials it needs for survival, so we need to draw in some feelings— empathy, affection, joy, peace, gratitude, self-esteem, healthy forms of guilt and grief, and the list goes on—as essential ingredients that help us survive as Christians—and as humans. We take these feelings into our hearts, and they give us life. They make us who we are.

If we embrace a feeling that should stay, our hearts will digest it, using its energy to move us forward in life, in faith, in love. The Bible tells us, "The fruit of the Spirit is love, joy, peace, patience, kindness, goodness, faithfulness, gentleness and self-control. Against such things there is no law" (Galatians 5:22-23). The Spirit produces both character traits and emotions in us. The more we stay in step with the Spirit, the more our emotional life will reflect the Spirit's fruit.

But some of the feelings that make it into our hearts should only come in temporarily—and others (ideally) should not enter at all. When a feeling enters our hearts and we know it can't stay, we have to deal with it. Such feelings must be ejected through prayer and a determined, deliberate thought life.

## HERE'S THE DOOR . . .

So let's say you've heard about a Sad Thing someone else is going through and you've allowed their pain to cross your emotional membrane. They feel sad, and you feel sad for them. Now what? Here's the tricky skill we all have to learn: *once we let someone else's pain in, after a while, we have to let it back out.*

I can hear your skeptical question: *And exactly how do I do that?*

Let's go back to our microscopic friends for more counsel. Material that enters a cell can come in both passively and actively. Some materials cross the membrane almost automatically, without attraction or invitation on the cell's part (passive transport). Other material has to be deliberately invited in by the cell (active transport). In my experience, the darker emotions—discouragement, depression, regret—seem to pass more readily through my membrane. They cross the threshold of my heart without any invitation on my part—they just show up at the door, waltz inside, and say, "Hey, dinner smells good!" While the dark feelings let themselves in without knocking, I often have to deliberately invite, and sometimes coax, the lighter ones—joy, love, peace—to come in and hang out with me.

So emotions may enter us passively or actively: sometimes with our invitation, sometimes without. But here's a fascinating fact (and I promise we're not just having fun with science; this has a practical application): when a cell has to eject material, it almost always ejects it actively. Excess or toxic material rarely leaves passively, all on its own—the cell *forces it out.*

Sounds awfully familiar to the way our emotions work, doesn't it? Some emotions enter us unconsciously; others enter when we invite them in; but they rarely leave on their own. (Have you ever sat around wishing your sadness would just go away?) If a particular feeling has outstayed its welcome, we have to deliberately send it away, like an uninvited houseguest or a nosy neighbor who has stayed too long.

What that means is:

Sadness will stick around . . . unless we make it leave.
Bitterness will linger . . . unless we drive it out.
Hopelessness will hang around . . . unless we send it on its way.

You may be thinking, *Okay, that makes sense, but* how *do I drive away unwanted emotions—especially the kind I've borrowed from other people?* The answer is surprisingly simple: we do it with prayer. Prayer and trust. I think of the process like this:

**Emotions in:** Maybe we welcomed certain feelings on purpose; maybe they sneaked in without our permission. Whichever way they arrived, now that they are here, they must either be absorbed or ejected.

**Emotions wrapped in prayer:** We pray about whatever burden we're carrying, asking God to handle it—to comfort and correct, to help and heal. We take God up on his generous offer to carry our burdens: "Give all your worries and cares to God, for he cares about you" (1 Peter 5:7, NLT).

**Emotions out:** Prayer carries the emotions and burden out—back across the membrane of our heart, outside our constant conscious attention—and places it in God's loving and capable care.

So what does this look like in the real world? You remember little Hunter's tragic story I told earlier in this chapter? I drive by his shrine almost every day. Now when I stop at Hunter's light, my eyes drift over to the ribbons and bears, the sign that reads, "Our Batman has wings." As always, my heart gives a familiar tug, and a bit of sadness drifts in. I don't fight it.

But then I start praying. I pray for Hunter's mother, his father, and all who loved him—who love him still. I pray they are healing. I pray God is helping them preserve the memory of his giggles, his smiles, the way his chubby arms felt around their necks. And even as they remember, I pray they can move forward—not *on*, but forward. I pray they will be able to resurrect joy—somehow, some way—in life and in their family.

The light turns green, and as Hunter's shrine grows small in the rearview mirror, I choose to leave his family where they belong: in the all-knowing, all-loving hands of the Father. Having done all I can for Hunter's family, I deliberately point my thoughts in a new direction. I either start a new conversation with someone riding in the car with me, or I pray about something or someone else.

This isn't a perfect solution, of course, but it does help. Prayer brings God into our emotional life. It helps us direct our thoughts and engage our faith, and in the end, it guides our feelings. It helps us share other people's loads for a time without taking them home to live with us forever.

## REMEMBER WHO THE SAVIOR OF THE WORLD IS . . . AND ISN'T

As we learn how to share others' burdens, let us never forget: there *is* someone who can carry all the burdens of all the people around the world, and that person is the triune God. Not me. Not you. Let us draw comfort and perspective from these great promises from Scripture:

He who sits on the throne
    will shelter them with his presence.
"Never again will they hunger;
    never again will they thirst.
The sun will not beat down on them,"
    nor any scorching heat.
For the Lamb at the center of the throne
    will be their shepherd;
"he will lead them to springs of living water."
    "And God will wipe away every tear from
        their eyes."

REVELATION 7:15-17

These words are life giving. Hope healing. All redeeming. God is on the job, ready to help and heal—*already* helping and healing. Ready to take on the world's burdens—carry them, heal them, wipe them away—as only he can.

## FEELING YOUR WAY FORWARD

### Prayer Prompt

My prayer is not for them alone. I pray also for those who will believe in me through their message, that all of them may be one, Father, just as you are in me and I am in you. May they also be in us so that the world may believe that you have sent me. I have given them the glory that you gave me, that they may be one as we are one—I in them and you in me—so that they may be brought to complete unity. Then the world will know that you sent me and have loved them even as you have loved me.

JOHN 17:20-23

## Journal Prompts

1. How do you know if you are overstepping the bounds of healthy compassion and sorrow sharing and entering the realm of burden borrowing? The distinction can be fuzzy at times, but here are a few telltale signs you might be a burden borrower:

   - You struggle to distinguish between your pain and someone else's.
   - When you grieve with others, you can't move on.
   - You try to fix people instead of inspiring or influencing them.
   - You feel guilty and responsible when someone else is spiritually wandering.
   - You become overwhelmed by social media and the news. Bad news or a sad post can send you spiraling downward.
   - You feel guilty when someone else is hurting, as though their pain were your fault—or as though you shouldn't experience any joy while someone else is hurting.
   - You try to do for people what they can only do for themselves.
   - You try to do for people what only God can do for them.
   - You are often a dumping ground for other people's feelings.

   Which of these burden-borrowing traits do you struggle with most?

2. How can you continue to love others and share their burdens without borrowing their pain in unhealthy ways?

3. What one thing could you do differently to lighten the burden you carry?

# CHAPTER 9

# CYNICISM: (TOO) GREAT EXPECTATIONS

I have often thought to myself, *The trouble is, I'm such an optimist, it's making me a pessimist.* We big feelers see what can be, what (in our humble opinion) *should* be. Our expansive imaginations envision high-definition, Technicolor scenarios that make real life, with all its imbalance and imperfection, fade into grainy black and white.

We don't just think *marriage*; we think *Mr. Darcy striding across a sleepy field at dawn, whispering, "I couldn't sleep because I love-I-love-I-love you, and by the way, I have ten thousand pounds a year and a ginormous estate."* (*Pride and Prejudice*, anyone? The 2005 movie version?) We don't just think *church*; we think *God's close-knit people dwelling in blissful harmony with no drama while everyone holds hands and sings—well, not "Kumbaya," because this isn't 1976, but probably some song by Lauren Daigle.* We don't just think *pastor*; we think *perfect leader who connects with every member (especially me) on a personal level, anticipates every need, and gives inspiring sermons that make us laugh while gently nudging us forward in spiritual growth.*

And then there is our sometimes-a-gift, sometimes-a-curse attention to detail: we can spot every flaw, notice every negative nuance, and hone in on the one unhappy person in the room. And if noticing weren't painful enough, then comes the kicker: we feel like someone must fix the problem—namely, us.

How wild we dream, how high our hopes fly. And when those dream-bubbles burst, when our hope-kites come crashing down, strings all a-tangle, we are left disillusioned at best, soul-wounded at worst. If we're not careful, our expectations can collapse into cynicism and bitterness. The glass isn't just half-empty; we're not sure we can trust the glass to hold water at all.

## HOPE IN THE FACE OF DISAPPOINTMENT

This world can be a hard place for big feelers—even a dangerous place. And although big feelers may fall prey to disappointment more often than others, steady and reluctant feelers suffer their share of lost hopes too, and when that happens, we all must resist cynicism. It comes to this: we have to learn to face the real without losing our ideals. To keep wild-dreaming even as we live in a world that often seems bent on killing the dreamer.

In this struggle we find a kindred spirit in the apostle Paul. No one knew the struggles of the early believers better than Paul, who had devoted his life to planting and strengthening churches. Paul loved God's people fiercely: "I face daily the pressure of my concern for all the churches," he wrote to the dysfunctional congregation in Corinth. "Who is weak, and I do not feel weak? Who is led into sin, and I do not inwardly burn?" (2 Corinthians 11:28-29).

Let's take a look at a time when Paul's visions and love for the church were tested.*

---

* This scene is based on Paul's letter to the Philippian church.

Paul leans his head against the cold stone wall. He groans and stretches rusty limbs as far as the chains will allow. It's never far enough, never a full stretch. He aches down to the bone—here a dull throb, the memory of a broken rib in Lystra; there a sharp pain, a still-healing wound from the previous week.

Eyes squeezed shut, he begins moving his lips in silent prayer. He's been praying his way through the churches—where did he stop this morning? *Ah, yes. Philippi.* His lips pull into a smile. *Oh, Lord, how can I thank you enough for—*

The door opens with a clank.

Paul jerks upright, blinking in the semi-dark. A figure, fuzzy around the outlines, enters. He crosses the cell in three steps and thrusts something into Paul's hand. Up close, Paul can make it out: a plate with food. Paul squints up at the face; his eyes strain to draw the features into focus. "Thank you."

"Eat the bread," the guard grunts, glancing over his shoulder toward the door. "It's fresh."

Paul picks up the bread and gives it a squeeze—hard as bone. He taps it against the plate—*tick, tick, tick*—and gives a bemused smile. "If this is fr—" The guard gives Paul a silencing look. He flicks one finger toward Paul's plate, and Paul follows the motion. His heart gives a hiccup.

A bit of folded parchment rests on the plate where the bread had been.

"Eat fast, wretch, or I'll mix it with your filth." The soldier speaks loudly, his words directed toward the door.

Paul snatches up the parchment and tucks it into his tattered sleeve with fumbling fingers. He gives the soldier a small smile as a silent thank-you.

The man nods. "I *told* you to hurry up!" he shouts, looking over his shoulder again. Clapping his palms together—*slap*—he dumps the rest of the food—a handful of old grapes, something green and wilted—into Paul's lap and clangs the plate hard against the stone wall. The ringing pierces Paul's ears and echoes through half the prison. The guard barks a too-loud laugh. "Take that, you insolent Jew."

From down the hall, Paul hears cackles of laughter and whoops of approval—whether from other soldiers or fellow prisoners, he's not sure. *Probably both,* he thinks with a wry smile.

As the soldier backs out, plate in hand, he mouths *sorry* with a guilt-wrinkled brow. Paul waves off the apology. Then he presses his palms together and bows his head in a gesture of gratitude.

When the bars clang shut, he digs the parchment from his sleeve, hoping the letters are large enough for him to make out with his poor vision.

*Our dear brother Paul,*

*Grace and peace. The brothers are preaching more than ever, and every week new believers are born again. Some are preaching because they are inspired by your example, but be warned: a few jealous troublemakers are speaking nearby, drawing as much attention as they can and riling up the soldiers. Be careful, brother. Trouble is coming. Stay strong. God be with you.*

The note is unsigned.

Paul folds the parchment and tucks it inside his robe, close to his heart. He sighs, waves of conflicting emotions jostling for attention. Gratitude. Affection. Fear. Hurt. And—this he hates to admit—resentment.

He leans back against the stone wall. He breathes in the musty air—wet soil, moldy rock, his own waste.

Heart burning, he prays, *I am afraid, but you are with me. What an honor to share in the sufferings of my Lord. To taste the betrayal he felt when he was kissed by a friend. To think that even this, this preaching from jealous hearts, will be for your glory! That it will bring new sons and daughters into your Kingdom. Because of this, I rejoice.* As his lips shape the words, his heart swells to meet them. His resentment eases. His courage rises and builds.

The latch rattles; Paul's eyes fly open with the door. A hulking shape fills the entrance. From where he sits, Paul can't make out the face, but he can tell that this man is twice the size of the soldier who delivered the note, and he can see the club being tossed from hand to hand. He can hear the smack of the wood as it hits one palm, then the other; he can hear the hiss of the soldier's eager breathing. He can smell the man's sweat, made more pungent by his twisted excitement.

"Your followers are causing trouble again," sneers the soldier. "Let's see what we can do about that."

"Hello, friend," Paul says. His muscles tense, but he feels no fear.

\* \* \*

This is my take on the events Paul describes in his letter to the church in Philippi. He writes from prison, in chains.[10] With Paul in jail, some believers had stepped up their preaching—not because they wanted to save souls, but because they wanted to make prison life harder for Paul. Jealous of his position, influence, and ministry success, they hoped to get him in trouble—to see him beaten, starved, abused.

Talk about a personal blow! Something that could wreck your faith in *all* people—and especially God's people. A betrayal like that could sour your faith, warp your perspective, calcify your heart. It could turn you into a skeptic, a cynic, a self-protective isolationist.

But did Paul allow that to happen? No. Fettered though his body was, his heart expressed unfettered affection for the Philippian church: "In all my prayers for all of you, I always pray with joy. . . . I have you in my heart. . . . I long for all of you with the affection of Christ Jesus" (Philippians 1:4, 7-8). Rather than lamenting the failings of a few, he focused on love. He trusted that God is greater than people's sins. He found good in evil, uncovered the blessing in a would-be curse: "The important thing is that in every way, whether from false motives or true, Christ is preached. And because of this I rejoice" (verse 18).

## THE GOD OF SECOND CHANCES

As he grappled with the injustice of being thrown in prison and the added insult of being backstabbed by fellow believers, Paul reflected the generous heart of God. Our God: stubborn in love, eternal in hope, relentless in forgiveness. The inventor of the second chance, the third chance, the seventy-times-seven (and on into infinity) chance. A Father who waits on the porch for his wayward child to slump back home, broke and broken. A Father who comes running and hugging and interrupting the apology speech to shower the unworthy prodigal with jewels (see Luke 15:20-24).

A Father Jesus describes like this:

> You have heard that it was said, "Love your neighbor and
> hate your enemy." But I tell you, love your enemies
> and pray for those who persecute you, that you may be

children of your Father in heaven. He causes his sun
to rise on the evil and the good, and sends rain on the
righteous and the unrighteous.

MATTHEW 5:43-45

Our God: gift giver, rain sender, sin forgetter. He showers us all
with rain and sunbeams, though we don't deserve it. Every day he
brings beauty to this imperfect world. He offers love to the sinful.
He interrupts our apologies before we're half-finished.

With this in mind, shouldn't we forgive others—and
ourselves—as the Lord does when we fall short? Yes. Shouldn't we
love others even when they don't live up to our expectations? Yes.
Shouldn't we embrace life and beauty on this maddening planet?
Yes. God's example helps us to stop waiting for perfect and just
focus on extending our love. It helps us to love as he does: without
strings, without concern for the final result.

## KEEP DREAMING

When we envision beauty and long for near-impossible circumstances, we are not naive, stupid, or gullible. When we ache and
yearn and dream, we are like him. We echo the heartbeat of the
one who set our own hearts beating. When we dream of what
could be—what should be—in this world, in the church, and in
our relationships, we are daring to envision heaven, striving to
capture a piece of it in our hearts if not in our hands.

Our God is a dreamer. He is the original perfectionist—he *is*
perfect. Perfect in love, perfect in life. The original idealist—*the*
ideal. He's everything we ought to be and long to be.

When God spoke the world into being, when he saw the
perfection he'd made, he said, "It is good . . . very good" (see
Genesis 1:31). Talk about the understatement to outdo all
understatements!

When he dreamed of his relationship with his children, his heart sang this song:

"How gladly would I treat you like my children
    and give you a pleasant land,
the most beautiful inheritance of any nation."
    I thought you would call me "Father"
    and not turn away from following me.
JEREMIAH 3:19

Like us, God experienced disappointment and hurt:

"Like a woman unfaithful to her husband,
    so you, Israel, have been unfaithful to me,"
    declares the LORD.
JEREMIAH 3:20

But he kept loving anyway. And loves to this day—arms stretched wide, heart left vulnerable.

I urge you to be like God as you keep dreaming, as you keep believing. Don't let your longing for beauty and perfection tarnish with time, even as you accept that many dreams can only be fully realized in heaven. One day every knee will bow. Every wrong will be righted. Every tear will be dried. Every broken body will be raised and restored. One day the whole world will cry, "Glory."[11]

Until that day, let us live in the real world—eyes and heart open, claiming joy where we can. But let us keep dreaming too. Let our feet walk this earth even as our eyes search the sky and our hearts await heaven.

As C. S. Lewis writes,

If I find in myself a desire which no experience in this world can satisfy, the most probable explanation is that

I was made for another world. . . . I must take care, on the one hand, never to despise, or be unthankful for, these earthly blessings, and on the other, never to mistake them for the something else of which they are only a kind of copy, or echo, or mirage. I must keep alive in myself the desire for my true country, which I shall not find till after death; I must never let it get snowed under or turned aside; I must make it the main object of life to press on to that other country and to help others to do the same.[12]

## FEELING YOUR WAY FORWARD

### Prayer Prompt

The LORD is compassionate and gracious,
  slow to anger, abounding in love.
He will not always accuse,
  nor will he harbor his anger forever;
he does not treat us as our sins deserve
  or repay us according to our iniquities.
For as high as the heavens are above the earth,
  so great is his love for those who fear him;
as far as the east is from the west,
  so far has he removed our transgressions from us.
As a father has compassion on his children,
  so the LORD has compassion on those who fear him;
for he knows how we are formed,
  he remembers that we are dust.

PSALM 103:8-14

## Journal Prompts

1. In which areas do you struggle most with cynicism: Relationships? The church? Your view of yourself? The world in general? Why are those areas so difficult for you?

2. Describe a time when God gave you a second chance. How can you extend that kind of grace to others—or to yourself?

3. How can you imitate Paul's decision to seek God's greater purposes in the midst of unfair suffering?

4. What do you most look forward to about heaven? How does it comfort you in the midst of present disappointments to anticipate the beautiful life that awaits you—a life free from sin, sorrow, and sickness?

# CHAPTER 10

# IDEALISM: FINDING JOY IN THE MIDST OF IMPERFECTION

My friend speaks through an apologetic laugh: "I just can't stop thinking that while we sit here, every minute ten thousand gallons of oil are spilling into the ocean. Killing fish, destroying reefs . . ." She tapers off into a sigh, tries to bury it in a laugh. "Sorry. We were talking about books and here I am, Debbie Downer. I just wish they'd hurry and get that pipeline plugged up."

She changes the topic, and I go along. But I am not fooled. I see the strain in her eyes, hear the tautness in her voice, sense the sorrow streaming just beneath the surface, almost like the sludge that's spilling into the ocean she loves. In the silence I hear the words she doesn't say: *How can I do life—drink coffee, make small talk—while this disaster continues?* And I know exactly what she means.

**You might be an idealist if . . .**

1. Life rarely lives up to your expectations.

2. You often feel disappointed by circumstances, other people, or yourself.

3. You struggle to shake one bad thing in an otherwise great day.

4. You often feel let down by other people.

5. You are rarely satisfied with your own work, performance, or character.

6. You have "splinter thoughts" that won't go away: one small, negative thought gets under your skin—irritating, distracting, tormenting—and you can't let it go.

7. You often begin sentences by saying, "Well, it would have been great, but . . ."

Joy and grief, oil and water—surely they can never marry. Doesn't life have to be flawless before joy is possible? We sensitive, big-feeling types struggle with stubborn idealism, and we have already discussed the need to guard against cynicism. But it's more than just disillusionment we wrestle with: it's discouragement. Frustration. Stolen joy. We have difficulty accepting imperfections in life, in relationships, and in ourselves. Life stymies our expectations with its confusing, plot-twisting, gut-wrenching turns. Every day is an infuriating, intoxicating mix of heartache and hilarity and holy mess. And sensitive souls struggle to process the mix.

If you ask a big feeler how their day was, they might say something like, "Everything would have been great, but then there was this one thing . . ." We struggle to move past the One Imperfect Thing—it feels dishonest. As long as there are hard things—even one hard thing—how can we allow ourselves to be happy? If life is not all delight all day long, it's a disappointing disaster. The same holds true for our spiritual life: if we aren't sinless saints, we're wretched souls condemned to hell. There's no middle ground.

Is it possible to adjust our perspective and expectations so that we not only avoid cynicism but also find peace and happiness even when life is imperfect? And if so, how? Let's begin by looking at the big picture with a wide lens. Whatever kind of feeler you are, we all have times when we need to adjust our expectations in order to cope with life's complexities. First we'll seek strategies for hanging on to joy and peace when the world is a mess, and then we'll zoom in to talk about dealing with imperfections in our own character and relationships.

## JOY IN ONE HAND, GRIEF IN THE OTHER

What is an idealist to do with this messy world we live in? Every time a bomb falls, a child gets cancer, or a tornado strikes, your joy takes a hit. Even if you try to move forward, go on with your day, it's there—a splinter in your mind. *As long as this Horrible Thing is happening out there, how can I be happy in my little life? I have no right to joy when others are suffering!*

The Bible acknowledges the complex emotional dance we so often fumble through, that feeling of misalignment that comes when our desires are out of sync with reality: "Even in laughter the heart may ache, and rejoicing may end in grief" (Proverbs 14:13). How grateful I am for this honesty! I, too, have struggled to laugh in the middle of heartache, to rejoice knowing grief lurks just around the corner.

### Jesus' Example

No one knew more about the sorrows of life, the brokenness of this sin-saturated world, than Jesus, the man of sorrows. He who had walked heaven end to end, who rejoiced as God called the first star to shine and the new earth to spin, who once joined in the angels' song—oh, he knew perfection. He had tasted perfection—he had breathed it, authored it, even taken on human form to model perfect love here on earth—but his reception by his own creation was far from perfect. Far from what he deserved. *He was in the world*—this world he had called forth from the void and nurtured from dust—*and the world knew him not.*\*

And yet Jesus found joy even here on this fractured planet, this place where cancer kills and oil spills, where boyfriends lie and babies die. Here in this darkness, he shone light, he enjoyed light—more, he *was* light. He made room to celebrate and be celebrated.

Let's drop into a scene that occurred shortly before Jesus' death. Although at first glance this interaction has little to do with idealism, it can help us address it in a roundabout way.

Jesus' impending suffering haunts his thoughts, an ever-present specter, but to the end his disciples, future-blind, carry on as if they have all the time in the world: eating dinner, swapping stories, arguing over which of them is the greatest.

Shortly before the Last Supper, they all go to dinner at the home of a man named Simon the Leper. A woman honors Jesus with a gift of astounding generosity. She pours a jar of perfume—worth a year's wages for a day laborer, most likely a family heirloom—onto his head.

Some at the dinner are appalled: "What a waste!" they grumble. "This perfume could have been sold and the money donated—it could have fed a poor family for weeks."

But Jesus' response is extraordinary (and here I quote the NIV word for word): "Why are you bothering this woman? She has done a beautiful thing to me. The poor you will always have with you, but you will not always have me. When she poured this perfume on my body, she did it to prepare me for burial. Truly I tell

---

\* John 1:10, KJV

you, wherever this gospel is preached throughout the world, what she has done will also be told, in memory of her."*

Consider these words: *The poor you will always have with you.* It's a strange line coming from Jesus, isn't it? We half-expect Jesus to take a different path—a path that would seem more righteous. We unconsciously anticipate the scene going more like this:

> The disciples object. The woman shrinks back. Jesus says, "Yes, brothers, of course you're right. We shouldn't waste precious resources on lavish gestures—and certainly not on ourselves." He extends a kind but mildly reproving smile to the woman. "I so appreciate your intent, but your generosity is misdirected. I'd rather you not waste such an expensive gift on me. Give it to those who really need it."

But here Jesus—huge-hearted Jesus, not-so-rich-himself Jesus, always-elbow-deep-in-comforting-the-needy Jesus—was essentially saying, "The world's poverty problem isn't going anywhere. Inequality will remain until I return and make things new. Even so, we don't have to allow our every interaction to be darkened by it. Yes, there are poor people in the world—no one knows this better than I do—and one day I will return and set things right. But until then, we can still celebrate moments of beauty. We can—and sometimes should—give gifts beyond reason. We should love past 'responsible.'"

In this tender scene, Jesus acknowledged the ever-present nature of suffering—not just the suffering of the poor, but his own impending agony—and then set it aside for a few precious

---

* Matthew 26:8-13

hours. He was able to receive love and honor and an over-the-top gift with gratitude and grace.

This scene helps idealists like us because it allows us to take a step back and see the big picture—the eternal picture. It shows us that we can enjoy life even in the presence of heartache and hurt. No, we don't turn a blind eye to pain; no, we don't ignore it, but it doesn't have to dominate our every meal, our every conversation, our every thought. We can make friends, give gifts, tell jokes, and savor joy, even as pain marches on.

## REWRITING THE HAPPY RULES

But what about when heartache and imperfection are not a world away, not "out there," nameless and faceless—but are right here? In our own lives, with our own people? Let's set aside large-scale suffering for a moment to talk about disappointments in daily life, because let's be honest: our days aren't always polluted by Big Philosophical Questions and Pains. Sometimes we're plagued by small things, trifling troubles—the "little foxes that ruin the vine-yards" (Song of Songs 2:15).

I can't tell you how many times my happy train has been derailed by One Bad Thing—one kind-of-stupid, shouldn't-be-earth-shattering thing. The day may be going swimmingly, my expectations are high (way higher than they should be, of course), and *bam*. One snippy word, one off-kilter interaction, one awkward exchange, and down starts the spiral. It's like a nail in the tire of my joy ride, leaking the happy out till the car sits lopsided on the side of the road. Down goes the day. And if the One Bad Thing involves my feeling like I sinned in some way— oh, heaven help us all. The guilt hangs around like an itchy tag on the back of my shirt—always there, always irritating, always just out of reach.

If you're a sensitive type, you know what I mean. It only takes one thing to set us off. A single thing goes awry, and we struggle to let it go. The whole conversation, the whole day, the whole vacation—even our whole life, if we are having a particularly dramatic moment—is now ruined. Or if not ruined, it's at least cast in shadow. No wonder we look at our peppy, carefree friends with envy and awe: *How do they do it? How do they stay joyful in the face of imperfection?*

These next words have come after years—decades, actually—of pillow pounding and prayer wrestling. I do not write them lightly, because they aren't easy to accept, and they are even more difficult to put into practice. But here's the truth: we must learn to be happy even when we are sad. Even when our life, our day, our relationships, and even our own hearts, are imperfect.

We all have unconscious "rules for happiness" in the back of our minds:

> I can't be happy unless my boyfriend/spouse/best friend/child
>   is happy.
> I can't be happy until I'm married.
> I can't be happy until I have a baby.
> I can't be happy until I lose five pounds.
> I can't be happy until I'm healthy again.
> I can't be happy until I'm out of debt.
> I can't be happy unless my work is going well.
> I can't be happy until my child comes back to God.

If we want to claim joy in the midst of this messy life, we have to rewrite our own rules for happiness, the rules by which we limit ourselves (not to mention God). If you search your heart, you may find that you unconsciously adhere to some happiness rules that sound something like this:

I can finally be happy when . . .
Life will be peaceful when . . .
My life will be good when . . .

But what if the *when* you're waiting for never comes? Will you postpone joy indefinitely? What if you rewrote your rules for happiness like this:

I can be joyful even though . . .
God can give me peace even while . . .
My life is already good in spite of . . .

We have to stop waiting for perfect before we allow ourselves to be happy. If we wait for a perfect day to be happy, we may never experience another happy day in life!

Scripture gives us another alternative: to embrace a kind of joy that defies our circumstances.

> Though the fig tree does not bud
>     and there are no grapes on the vines,
> though the olive crop fails
>     and the fields produce no food,
> though there are no sheep in the pen
>     and no cattle in the stalls,
> yet I will rejoice in the Lord,
>     I will be joyful in God my Savior.
>
> HABAKKUK 3:17-18

## THE POWER OF A DO-OVER

Remember do-overs from your playground days? Was the ball fair or foul? Nobody knows? *Do-over!* Somebody trips during dodge-ball and gets hit while they're down and they don't think it was fair and now they're crying? *Do-over!* Jesus says we need to become like little children—and I suspect their resilience is one admirable trait he had in mind. Why can't grown-ups also apply the do-over principle? After years of self-torment over imperfect days, imperfect interactions, and an imperfect *me*, I've learned to embrace do-overs in my life and relationships.

If we can teach ourselves to capture the little "off" moments and deal with them—apologize as needed, rectify what we can as fast as we can—and then move forward with a clean slate, what a different life we can lead! A freed-up life. A life that doesn't have to be perfect in order to be enjoyed.

What does this look like in the real world? Here is a classic example from my own marriage. My husband and I don't argue very often, but when we do, it often goes something like this. (Yes, our primary topic of argument is usually calendars—I can't decide if I am embarrassed or proud of that fact.)

\* \* \*

Kevin walks into the kitchen and spies me locked in a staring contest with my computer screen. "Could we sit down and talk through our week?"

I look up, squinting. My eyes are pointed at my husband, but they're still seeing all the adverbs I need to delete. "Huh?"

Kevin waves his calendar in the air and gestures toward the couch. He points at me, then points at himself, and mimes sitting down.

"Now?" My eyes focus, home in on his thin black calendar. I glare at it, envisioning all the boxes and lines on its pages—all the time commitments and to-dos they represent. I feel a burst of adrenaline. It's fight or flight time—I choose flight. My brain offers up a half-dozen desperate escape routes: *I have a deadline. I have emails to send. I feel the measles coming on.*

Kevin nods. "Now would be great."

I grip my ergonomic mouse tight, as if it can save me. "Why now? I have five million things—"

"Exactly! If we don't do it now, the week will start flying and we'll be sprinting in different directions, each doing our five million things. It'll only take ten minutes, I promise."

I snort. "Ten minutes? Yeah, right. You always say that, then we always end up sitting there for an hour." I drill him with my *you know I'm right* stare.

"Fifteen minutes. And you can drink coffee." Kevin flashes a wheedling sideways grin, the one little boys give their mothers to say, *I'm so cute, don't you want to let me have my way?*

I shake my head, flash him a look that says, *I'm on to you— you may be cute, but that smile doesn't work on me.* "I know how this goes. One minute we're talking about this Thursday; the next you're making me map out the entire year. I don't want to start planning Thanksgiving and Christmas. It's *February.*"

"Who said anything about Thanksgiving and Christmas? We just need to talk through this week." He looks down and mumbles to his socks, "And maybe the next month or two. And maybe Thanksgiving for two minutes."

"Aha!" I crow, triumphant. "You *are* trying to trick me. You and your evil calendars and your nefarious need to obsessively plan life three years in advance. I don't even know what I'm making for dinner tonight. If you make me think about all the things we have to do next month, let alone next fall, my brain will explode. Actually explode. Like, brain matter all over the kitchen." I make an exploding sound and wiggle my fingers around my head.

Now it's Kevin's turn to make the your-efforts-at-cuteness-are-lost-on-me face. "Elizabeth, we have to plan things. Calendars are not evil; they're a part of life."

"Not *my* life. Not if I don't want them to be. And certainly not right now while I'm trying to write. I have adverbs to delete! Passive voice to flip around! Besides, Jesus never had a calendar." These last words come out sharper than I intended—I meant to make a joke.

Irritation irons Kevin's smile out flat. He starts backing away, palms up. "Fine. Forget I brought it up."

Regret rises. Within seconds, I'm cowering beneath a towering tsunami of impending guilt. I bury my face in my hands and groan. "Fine. I'll do it. I'm sorry. I didn't mean to be mean."

Kevin grunts, "It's fine." But he doesn't sound fine; he sounds hurt.

The tsunami drags me under, rolls me around. "Ugh, no, it's not fine. I snapped at you, and I'm sorry."

Kevin sighs, sounding less hurt, more like himself: "It *is* fine. I know you hate calendars. And I shouldn't have sneaked up on you when you were writing."

I sniff. "Now I can't even think about the calendar. I feel like I ruined our whole day." In the tsunami's wake, a dark cloud of guilt has mushroomed and parked over my head.

"How about we have a do-over? Pretend that whole conversation never happened and try it again?"

I shrug.

Kevin gives a playful smile and backs across the room, as if rewinding himself. At the doorway, he starts walking forward again. "My lovely wife, my sweet and flexible and always pleasant and organized wife, pardon the heinous interruption. I know you are engaged in a battle with adverbs, but could you please consider taking a break so we can sit down and talk through our week?"

Begrudgingly, I smile. The guilt cloud thins. Kevin gives his calendar a little shake, holding it out and waving his other hand around it like one of those game show models trying to make cheap prizes look appealing. A laugh escapes my mouth even as I roll my eyes. The cloud evaporates to misty remnants. "Yes. Give me a minute to grab a cup of coffee, and I'll come sit with you."

Kevin smiles. "What a wonderful person you are! Why, you are so wonderful, I'll even warm up your coffee for you!" He mumbles the last words in a rush: "Especially if you take two minutes to look ahead to holiday plans." He gives a hopeful, toothy grin.

I stand up and flash him a don't-push-it look. "Do-over or no do-over, I'm still not talking about Thanksgiving. It's February."

"Can we at least plan Easter? Father's Day?" He wiggles his eyebrows. "*Mother's* Day?"

I shake my head and sock him in the shoulder. "I'll look ahead three weeks. That's it. Brain matter all over the kitchen, remember." Another exploding sound.

Kevin smiles. "I had to try."

\* \* \*

Welcome to our marriage. Kevin and I introduced do-overs to our relationship years ago, and what a life-saver—and a joy-saver—they have been! As someone who struggles to release guilt and negativity, I find that the do-over provides a fresh start when I've been less than who I want to be. It helps me give myself permission to let go and move forward, forgiving myself and others. It reminds me that a day is composed of twenty-four hours, and a few bad minutes don't need to taint the rest of the day.

Do-overs may be a modern word borrowed from the

playground, but they are a biblical concept. God is the original author of do-overs:

> Forget the former things;
>     do not dwell on the past.
> See, I am doing a new thing!
>     Now it springs up; do you not perceive it?
> I am making a way in the wilderness
>     and streams in the wasteland. . . .
>     to give drink to my people, my chosen,
> the people I formed for myself
>     that they may proclaim my praise.
>
> ISAIAH 43:18-19, 20-21

My fellow idealist, if you struggle to release negative moments and move forward, give do-overs a try. It's true that some things can't be taken back—some words leave a permanent mark, and some actions result in painful consequences. But in some situations, do-overs can help us get unstuck; they can help us reframe a situation.

Try them in your walk with God. If you sin, ask him for forgiveness and a fresh start, then trust that in his kindness, he will grant your request.

Try them in your friendships. If you have an awkward moment, apologize quickly and ask your friend to let you rephrase and try again.

Try them in your dating relationship or marriage. You may not argue about calendars like my husband and I do, but if you do, do-overs may save the day while you save the dates.

Try them in your parenting. Oh, what a blessing do-overs are in dealing with children! Kevin and I use them all the time with our four kids. They allow us to offer our kids swift grace, with no time spent in the doghouse. (And do-overs go both ways: they allow our kids to offer us grace too!) They allow our family to be imperfect and messy, even as we seek to grow in righteousness.

As much as perfection on earth is mere fantasy, it will be a daily reality in heaven. (And God's people said, "Amen!") But until heaven, we idealists have to find ways to cope with our imperfect circumstances and our imperfect faith lived alongside imperfect people packed onto an imperfect planet. Like Jesus, we have to look past heartache to live and love in the present. Like God, we need to love even when we've been disappointed. At times, we may even need to rewind and redo—and let others rewind and redo. Because if we don't get it perfect the first time—well, practice makes perfect.

## FEELING YOUR WAY FORWARD

### Prayer Prompt

Seventy years are given to us!
    Some even live to eighty.
But even the best years are filled with pain and trouble;
    soon they disappear, and we fly away. . . .

Satisfy us each morning with your unfailing love,
    so we may sing for joy to the end of our lives.
Give us gladness in proportion to our former misery!
    Replace the evil years with good.
Let us, your servants, see you work again;
    let our children see your glory.

PSALM 90:10, 14-16, NLT

## Journal Prompts

1. Fill in the blank with some of the "happiness rules" you have made for yourself:

   I can finally be happy when . . .
   Life will be peaceful when . . .
   My life will be good when . . .

   Now try reframing those sentences:

   I can be joyful even though . . . because . . .
   God can give me peace even while . . . because . . .
   My life is already good in spite of . . . because . . .

2. In what relationship or setting could you give do-overs a try? How might do-overs change things for you?

3. Habakkuk 3:18 says, "I will rejoice in the LORD"; Paul tells us the same thing in Philippians 4:4: "Rejoice in the Lord always." What does it mean to rejoice "in the Lord"? How can we find joy in God even when life isn't at its most joyful—or isn't joyful at all?

# CHAPTER 11

# GUILT:
# WHAT IT DEMANDS FROM YOU

Of all the emotions, guilt is my least favorite—and yet in some seasons of my life, it has battered down my door and moved in as my constant companion. For my first few years as a Christian, I carried guilty feelings with me everywhere, like a weighted backpack. It was exhausting and overwhelming; not only did it rob me of joy, it robbed me of *life*. Maybe you, too, know what it's like to be plagued with relentless guilt. If so, I pray the words of this chapter will be a help and a balm to your aching heart.

Let's dive into this topic by exploring the life of Simon Peter. Hours after swearing to stand by Jesus even to death, Peter publicly denied his friend three times. He cursed and swore and reverted to the man he'd been before he met Jesus: Simon the weak, Simon the crass. Let's take a peek at what might have been going on in his mind as he confronted his guilt.

* * *

Peter can't escape the memory. It assaults him in disjointed images, like lightning flashes scalding his mind. The mottled face of the servant in the courtyard, turned his way. The firelight flickering in the man's eyes like serpent tongues. The crooked finger pointing, the harsh voice accusing: "This man was with him! He's a Galilean."

The eyes, so many eyes, turning on him, trapping him. The fear knotting his gut, crawling up his throat. The sound jerking out of his mouth—was it really his voice?—high, tight, afraid. The words, the awful words: "I don't know the man!" And the eyes of the Lord, the eyes of his friend, finding him even as he spoke—the eyes that were not angry, not surprised; just hurt. Sad.

And then in his memory he hears his own boasting, just hours earlier: *I am willing to die with you!*

Nausea slides through him, cold and twisting. He falls to his knees.

*Failure.*

*Coward.*

*Traitor.*

Sobs rack his body till no tears remain. He can't find words to pray, but something in him calls to God—a prayer without words, pleas without expectation. And a kind of answer comes: a memory.

Jesus' face in the lamplight—was it only last night?— the dark eyes shadowed, the young face lined with an old man's burdens. "You will all fall away . . . but I have prayed for you, Simon. When you have turned back, strengthen your brothers."

*When you have turned back.*

Not *if.*

*When.*

And something eases, ever so slightly, inside.

*He knew I would fail.*

*But he prepared a way back.*

*He believes I can come back.*

He sits up.

*And so I will.*

*I will.*

The gray of early morning has tipped toward blue.
Dawn is coming. He must go find his friend. Stand by him
for whatever comes next.

Peter made his way back to the Lord—first to the foot of the
cross, then to an empty tomb, and then to breakfast with Jesus
on a beach at dawn. Peter stood before his resurrected friend, and
Jesus—ever gracious, ever kind—gave him three opportunities to
recant his denials:

"Simon, do you love me?"

"Yes, Lord, you know that I love you."*

And instead of wallowing in guilt, Peter went on to lead power-
fully in the early church.

\* \* \*

Guilt holds the power to save or destroy, to lead us to redemption or drive us insane. So how do we develop the healthy kind of
relationship with guilt—the kind that moves us to change and leads
us to God? Let's consider what the Bible has to say.

---

* You can read the full story in John 21:15-25.

## BIBLICAL GUILT IS NOT A FEELING

In Scripture, guilt is not often referenced as a feeling, but rather as a condition. Guilt is a standing before God, a status in which we are responsible for wrongdoing and in need of forgiveness.

> If anyone sins and does what is forbidden in any of the LORD's commands, even though they do not know it, they are guilty and will be held responsible. They are to bring to the priest as a guilt offering a ram from the flock, one without defect and of the proper value. In this way the priest will make atonement for them for the wrong they have committed unintentionally, and they will be forgiven.
> LEVITICUS 5:17-18

> Jesus said, "If you were blind, you would not be guilty of sin; but now that you claim you can see, your guilt remains."
> JOHN 9:41

Do you see how the word *guilt* is used in these examples? (This is just a small sampling; there are many similar usages throughout the Bible.) The word does not communicate a *feeling* of guilt— a sense of shame and self-loathing—but rather a status we may occupy before God, a state that requires resolution, action.

And that distinction offers us a powerful, life-changing truth: guilt is not a feeling we are meant to live with forever; it's a problematic condition we're meant to resolve before God (or more accurately, a condition we need God to resolve for us through the blood of his Son).

## GODLY SORROW VERSUS WORLDLY SORROW

So what do we do when we sin? Paul's letters to the Corinthian church provide us with an excellent case study in how Christians should respond when they discover sin in their lives. The Corinthians had allowed sexual sin to go unchecked in their congregation, and Paul's previous letter, a scathing rebuke, prompted them to act. Paul comforted the penitent Corinthians with these words:

> Even if I caused you sorrow by my letter, I do not regret it. Though I did regret it—I see that my letter hurt you, but only for a little while—yet now I am happy, not because you were made sorry, but because your sorrow led you to repentance. For you became sorrowful as God intended and so were not harmed in any way by us. Godly sorrow brings repentance that leads to salvation and leaves no regret, but worldly sorrow brings death. See what this godly sorrow has produced in you: what earnestness, what eagerness to clear yourselves, what indignation, what alarm, what longing, what concern, what readiness to see justice done. At every point you have proved yourselves to be innocent in this matter. So even though I wrote to you, it was neither on account of the one who did the wrong nor on account of the injured party, but rather that before God you could see for yourselves how devoted to us you are. By all this we are encouraged.
>
> 2 CORINTHIANS 7:8-13

Scripture indicates there is a place for a godly kind of sorrow for sin—we can be "sorrowful as God intend[s]." But there's another kind of sorrow—a harmful kind that's not from God.

Paul—bless you for this, brother Paul—describes a dichotomy that simply begs to be put into chart form.

| GODLY SORROW | WORLDLY SORROW |
|---|---|
| Intended by God | Not intended by God |
| Hurts temporarily | Lasts too long |
| Brings repentance | Unproductive |
| Leaves no regret | Harmful |
| Leads to salvation | Brings death |

Godly sorrow, though it is painful for a time, brings healing and salvation in the end. It gives us the freedom to fully acknowledge and accept responsibility for our sins, but to do so in light of God's grace through the Cross. Yes, we have sinned; no, we don't deserve forgiveness, and no, we can't earn salvation—but God gives us grace. And grace doesn't ignore our sin, dress it up with flattering filters, or downplay its consequences. The staggering truth of grace is this: it is mighty enough to expose the enormity of our sin—the complete, honest, awful truth—and then to wash it all away. This grace is shocking, unexpected, almost incomprehensible. This grace is breathtaking, soul saving, overwhelming. And godly sorrow is the pathway to receiving that gift.

But worldly sorrow leads us along another path altogether. Worldly sorrow hurts us . . . and keeps hurting us. It keeps our thoughts focused not on God and his grace but on ourselves: *How could I sin like this? If I admit to this sin, then I'm worthless, a failure. I need to run from this . . . or justify myself . . . or try to earn God's forgiveness.* Such self-focused, merit-based thinking drives us further from God, further from grace.

To help us find the right path, Paul elaborates on some of the characteristics of godly sorrow. Let's take a closer look:

Earnestness: sincerity, truthfulness ("I'm not going to stretch the truth, sidestep responsibility, or avoid this situation.")

Eagerness to clear oneself: a genuine desire for resolution ("How can I make things right?")

Indignation: righteous anger at sin ("This is wrong. It violates God's ways.")

Alarm: recognition that this is serious ("Whoa! I can't ignore this.")

Longing: desire for connection ("I want to be right with God again. I want to be close to him.")

Concern: awareness of how your actions have affected God and others ("My sin has hurt other people; this isn't just about me.")

Readiness to see justice done: not shifting blame; willingness to make restitution or apology ("I'm ready to bear any consequences.")

What do all these characteristics have in common? They all lead to *action*. Yes, alarm and longing and concern are all emotions, but they are emotions with purpose and forward motion. They lead us to *do* something: repent. (Hold that thought—in a moment we're going to do a deeper dive on that oft-misunderstood word.)

Contrast these forward-moving emotions with the worldly side of the chart—the kind of sorrow that lasts too long, harms us emotionally and spiritually, and leads nowhere. I like to call worldly sorrow "wallowing," and oh, what a gifted wallower I am! If you need someone to show you how to sit around reliving a mistake on constant repeat, a boomerang video that loops and replays in your mind day after miserable day; if you need someone to model how to languish in self-loathing and despair, well, I'm your girl. At least I used to be, until I decided to—well, I decided to repent.

## DEMYSTIFYING REPENTANCE

Let's take a minute to explore the word *repent*. It's one of those churchy words that feels distant and formal—a word that should only be spoken from pulpits, right? But in reality, repentance is for all of us.

Repentance involves sorrow for sin, but it's so much more than that. Repentance is also an action, a decision. To repent means to change your mind—and change your direction.[13] Once we recognize and regret the error of our ways, we *change our ways*. John the Baptist said, "Produce fruit in keeping with repentance" (Luke 3:8). Repentance isn't just sitting around feeling bad; repentance bears the fruit of change in our lives.

God doesn't want us to lie around in sackcloth and ashes, eternally flogging ourselves over our mistakes. "I see that my letter hurt you," Paul wrote, "but only for a *little while*" (2 Corinthians 7:8, emphasis added). Sure, when first we recognize our sin, there's a place for short-term godly sorrow—alarm, concern, earnestness, and so on—but those feelings need to take us somewhere positive: to change.

Here's a litmus test that can help you evaluate whether guilty feelings are godly: *Once guilty feelings cease inspiring change and begin tormenting and disabling you, they have outlived their purpose.* They have jumped the line in the chart from godly sorrow to worldly sorrow. If you've already repented by making whatever changes you are able to make (recognizing that your growth may be imperfect and that some changes take time), and you still feel guilty, it's clear that inappropriate guilty feelings have taken root and need to be sent packing.

In the book of Acts, Peter describes the end result of repentance this way: "Repent, then, and turn to God, so that your sins may be wiped out, that times of refreshing may come from the Lord" (Acts 3:19). The Lord forgives us, then he gives us "times of refreshing":

joy, peace, freedom, a new start. *That's* what our loving God wants us to feel!

Before we go further, let's be clear on two things:

1. *Repentance doesn't earn forgiveness.* When I say we need to act when we sin, I don't mean to suggest that our actions in any way earn our forgiveness. Only Jesus' blood can earn forgiveness. But acting stands in contrast to simply sitting around feeling guilty, which can be paralyzing and debilitating. The longer we sit around wallowing in guilt, the less like Jesus we become. How does that honor God?

   And we shouldn't expect ourselves to repent perfectly (what does that even mean?). Repentance simply means we make a sincere effort to honor God and his ways as we move forward. We need grace *because* we are not perfect. That's why Jesus was the only one who could purchase grace on our behalf.

2. *We still stand in grace when we sin.* Once we become Christians, Jesus' grace is where we stand, where we live, and we can stand there in full confidence (see Hebrews 10:22). When my children make mistakes, I don't withdraw my love from them, and I certainly don't kick them out of my house. But in every family, hurt happens—sin happens—and relational restoration needs to take place through both apology and forgiveness.

   Similarly, we don't fall out of grace with God every time we fall—we are still totally saved and dearly loved. But we also don't want to cheapen God's grace by ignoring sin when we discover it ("Oh, well, no big deal—Jesus has that covered"). We want to acknowledge our sin to God and apologize, as we would in any other relationship.

Psalm 51 paints a beautiful picture of repentance in action. Written by David after the prophet Nathan exposed David's adultery and murder, it shows the humbled king's progression from sorrow and apology to change and—yes—joy.

He begins in the depths:

> Wash away all my iniquity
> and cleanse me from my sin.
> For I know my transgressions,
> and my sin is always before me.
> Against you, you only, have I sinned
> and done what is evil in your sight.
>
> PSALM 51:2-4

As the psalm continues, he progresses to transformation and restoration:

> Cleanse me with hyssop, and I will be clean;
> wash me, and I will be whiter than snow.
> Let me hear joy and gladness;
> let the bones you have crushed rejoice. . . .
>
> Restore to me the joy of your salvation
> and grant me a willing spirit, to sustain me.
>
> Then I will teach transgressors your ways,
> so that sinners will turn back to you.
>
> PSALM 51:7-8, 12-13

If David could be restored in his walk with God—beloved still, joyful again, useful once more—then surely you and I can experience the same healing and joy when we fall.

## WHAT DOES YOUR GUILT WANT?

Because I hate to feel guilty so much, I fear it. My instinct is to run away with my eyes squeezed shut and fingers plugging my ears, shouting, "I can't hear you! I'm not listening!" (Not a safe way to run, I know.) But I have learned a better way: to ask my guilt the simple question, "What do you want from me?" When I do, my fear fades and clarity comes. This question helps me to distinguish legitimate guilty feelings from false ones.

### Worldly Sorrow

False guilt (aka worldly sorrow) won't have anything useful to offer; it will just suggest things like, "I want you to hide in your room feeling like a worthless slug for the next three months. I want you to lose your confidence and stop using your gifts for God. And while we're at it, I want you to alienate your friends and family by becoming consumed with your own feelings." False guilt might say, "I want you to feel guilty and unworthy *all the time*—even when you can't identify an actual, identifiable sin in your life." When guilt responds that way, I realize it is worldly sorrow and it needs to hit the road.

Misplaced or exaggerated guilty feelings can be a tool Satan uses to torment us. He figures, "I can't trip her up with sin right now; I'll get her with excessive guilt instead!" Scripture acknowledges this struggle:

> Our actions will show that we belong to the truth, so we will be confident when we stand before God. Even if we feel guilty, God is greater than our feelings, and he knows everything.
>
> Dear friends, if we don't feel guilty, we can come to God with bold confidence. And we will receive from him whatever we ask because we obey him and do the things that please him.
>
> 1 JOHN 3:19-22, NLT

Sometimes our hearts need to be set at rest. Sometimes we feel guilty, but our feelings are wrong. "God is greater than our feelings, and he knows everything"—even the places in our own hearts we struggle to interpret.

## Godly Sorrow

On the other hand, when you ask legitimate guilt (aka godly sorrow), "What do you want?" it will have practical, purposeful actions in mind. Here are some biblical responses our legitimate guilty feelings may seek to prompt:

1. Turn to God with your sin (see Acts 3:19-20).
2. Seek forgiveness in prayer (see Luke 11:4).
3. Confess your sin to a trusted friend, seeking prayer and healing (see James 5:16).
4. Cut off sin, even if it means taking radical steps (see Matthew 5:27-30).
5. If you have sinned against another person, set things right as you are able (see Luke 19:8-10).

If your guilty feelings are prompting one of these responses, you will probably find that if you follow through, the guilty feelings will dissipate, replaced by joy and refreshment.

Here are a few principles to keep in mind as you grapple with guilt:

- God gives us guilty feelings (godly sorrow) to serve a purpose: to inspire change.
- When sorrow is godly, it nudges us toward change (repentance). It inspires us to be more like him.
- When sorrow is ungodly (worldly sorrow), it lasts too long and is emotionally harmful.

- Once guilty feelings cease inspiring change and begin tormenting and disabling, they have outlived their purpose and need to be sent packing.
- Healthy repentance should lead to joy and refreshment in the Lord.

## WHAT ABOUT CONSEQUENCES?

Many Christians live with long-term consequences from sin in their past. Every day they live with reminders of their past, repercussions from their sin, and sometimes those reminders feel like finger-pointing from God.

Let's not confuse *consequences* with *punishment*. God can totally love you—and use you to do great things for him—even as you live with lingering consequences from your past mistakes. Consider these examples from Scripture:

- Moses struck the rock, against God's specific command, so he wasn't able to lead the people into the Promised Land. He died before the Israelites crossed over into it. Even so, he continued to lead God's people and was honored in death as a great man of God. God did allow Moses to see the Promised Land from a distance before he died (see Numbers 20:1-13; Deuteronomy 34).
- After decades of infertility, decades of waiting for God to fulfill his promise that Abraham and Sarah would have a child, Sarah abandoned hope in God's plan and came up with a plan of her own. She urged Abraham to have a child with a concubine, Hagar. This decision resulted in heartache for Sarah and conflict in Sarah and Abraham's marriage. Even so, Sarah got to bear a baby boy, Isaac (see Genesis 16; 21).

Even though Christians are forgiven and free, we may live with some fallout from our decisions for the rest of our lives. Maybe an immoral past means you have some residual health issues or complex family dynamics; maybe selfish financial decisions mean that even though your debt with God is settled, your financial debts with other people remain. But you know what? That's okay. You are no less forgiven, no less loved than any other Christian. (Welcome to the We All Have Sinful Pasts Club. I have my membership card; you have yours.) If you've been washed in the blood of Christ, you can stand confidently in God's grace.

And guess what? Just like David and Peter, you may have to recover from colossal mistakes as a believer, and even after those sins are forgiven, they may carry consequences too. Even so, you can stand cleansed and confident in the grace of God, thanks to the blood of Christ.

## THE MAGNITUDE OF GRACE

At the risk of sounding ridiculously simple, I hope this chapter helps you begin to understand that God's grace is just so *big*. Bigger than all of us who rely on its saving power. Bigger than our little lives and our not-so-little sins.

Drink in these wondrous words about God's grace:

Since we have a great high priest who has ascended into heaven, Jesus the Son of God, let us hold firmly to the faith we profess. For we do not have a high priest who is unable to empathize with our weaknesses, but we have one who has been tempted in every way, just as we are— yet he did not sin. Let us then approach God's throne of grace with confidence, so that we may receive mercy and find grace to help us in our time of need.

HEBREWS 4:14-16

Thanks to Jesus, we can approach the throne of grace. Not the throne of power (though God is all-powerful) or the throne of fear (though God is fearsome)—the throne of *grace*. And we can approach that throne with confidence.

If guilty feelings have been hanging around like annoying neighbors who don't know when to go home, send them on their way. Grace is knocking too. Welcome it in and offer it a bedroom of its own. It's here to stay.

> Those whom I love I rebuke and discipline. So be earnest and repent. Here I am! I stand at the door and knock. If anyone hears my voice and opens the door, I will come in and eat with that person, and they with me.
>
> REVELATION 3:19-20

## FEELING YOUR WAY FORWARD

### Prayer Prompt

Blessed is the one
whose transgressions are forgiven,
whose sins are covered. . . .

I said, "I will confess
my transgressions to the LORD."
And you forgave
the guilt of my sin.

Therefore let all the faithful pray to you
while you may be found;
surely the rising of the mighty waters
will not reach them.
You are my hiding place;

you will protect me from trouble
and surround me with songs of deliverance.

PSALM 32:1,5-7

## Journal Prompts

1. Describe a time when you experienced the grace of God. What did grace feel like? How specifically did you experience it? How did it change you?

2. How does living in grace affect your relationship with God? Your relationship with other people?

3. Describe a time when you gave in to worldly sorrow. How did you feel, and how did those feelings affect your perspective, your relationships, and your effectiveness for God? Now describe a time when you sinned but repented with godly sorrow. How did you feel, and how did those feelings affect your perspective, your relationships, and your effectiveness for God?

4. How do you see God's grace at work even when you're dealing with the consequences of past sins? In what ways has God shown kindness to you? In what ways has he alleviated some of the hardships or heartache?

# PART THREE

# HOW DO EMOTIONS WORK IN THE REAL WORLD?

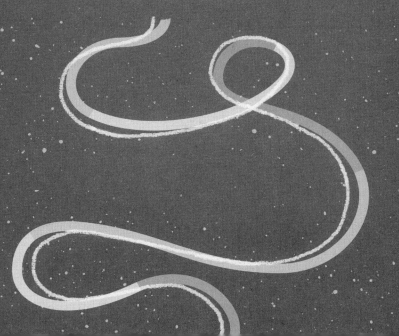

# CHAPTER 12

# THE POTENTIAL IN YOUR PRAYER LIFE

You steal away outside, and the evening sky steals your breath. Stars, so many stars—ancient diamonds scattered across velvet night. You are starstruck, dumbstruck, dizzy, and if you stare long enough, you see that the stars are stuttering, blinking. Somewhere in memory, you hear a teacher's voice saying that the light traveled tens of thousands of years before it arrived here to light this night, to touch your eyes. The world spins, and for a moment you almost see—sideways, like something caught at the edge of eyesight— how very small you are and how very great your God is. And in the silence, the stillness, he is, and you are, and it is very good.

\* \* \*

You sit quiet, blanket-wrapped, with a mug of steaming coffee. A dark room just before a winter dawn. In stumbles your little one:

dream-flushed cheeks, sleep-swollen eyes, bed-frizzed hair. Up she climbs for a morning snuggle, and you fold her in your arms and breathe her sacred, still-new-to-this-earth smell, and silently your heart sings to God, sings *with* God, celebrates this precious soul you share, this little one he designed and you get to raise. You beg his blessing and guidance and protection over her, and as night's stark black fades to new-day gray, you know he hears, and he cares. And as impossible as it feels, you know he loves her more than you do, and she is safe in his hands.

## EMOTIONS CAN CONNECT US WITH GOD

This is just a taste of the emotional communion we big feelers can experience in our walk with God. The constant conversation, the depth of connection, the sharing of life's moments, both great and small. The flight from heartache to ecstasy, joys both mighty and mundane—we can walk it all with God, *share* it all with God.

If the only style of prayer you've ever known is the scripted formulas we sometimes hear in church, or if your only personal prayer experience thus far has been reciting a rote prayer or offering God lists of thanks and wants and needs, oh, what joy still awaits you! What intimacy, what comfort, what thrill! There is more—so much more—to prayer, and I can't wait for you to discover this precious treasure. It's there for any and all who want to experience it—and you are invited.

Prayer is the only place where we can feel—and *be*—fully known. Where those deep feelings we have no words for can finally be expressed. And not just expressed, but understood.

## WHAT PRAYER CAN DO

In any relationship, conversation is only one part of our connection—but perhaps it is the most important part. And prayer is our part of the conversation with God. Prayer is an opportunity to connect with our perfect God, to share thoughts and emotions and experiences more honestly and intimately than any imperfect human relationship allows. Prayer is a safe place for pouring out our hopes and doubts and fears—pouring them into hands strong enough to hold them and kind enough to help them.

Prayer can be a transformative encounter. If we let God work, we come away forever changed. Prayer is not a wishing well, not a magic lamp—but it is the place where human struggles meet divine power. Prayer is more than a duty, more than a spiritual discipline—it is an invitation. An invitation from God to you.

Let's take a step back to consider the nature of God's offer—and how we begin to accept it through prayer. How do we describe the kind of relationship God invites us into? How can we cram the divine into the confines of human language? We'll do our best, knowing we'll never quite capture it.

## Prayer is an invitation to love and be loved.

> By day the LORD directs his love,
>> at night his song is with me—
>> a prayer to the God of my life.
>
> PSALM 42:8

To love and be loved: Isn't this the deep yearning of our existence? What we all want above all things? What every book, every story, every song, is about in the end? It's all about love.

And with God, we can have love. Perfect love. We can be so close to God that he fills us to the furthest reaches of these fathomless hearts of ours—these hearts he crafted in us to reflect *his* heart. Think of all that love we've poured out on the wrong people at times, leaving us feeling violated, taken for granted, betrayed. God is the one we can give it all to—he alone is worthy. Think of all the love we've yearned to feel from parents, teachers, friends, boyfriends, spouses, and all the wide world—that idealistic, perfect love we have eagerly searched for, quietly ached for, and sometimes embarrassed ourselves to earn or compromised ourselves to find. The search is over at last.

With God we can be known: truly, shockingly, nakedly known. No pretense, half-truths, or near-truths; no filters, fillers, or dyes. And it's okay that we are the imperfect partner in this relationship. Where we lack, he can forgive. Where we fail, he does not turn away. Where we wish we were different—more lovable—he loves anyway. He sees the person we *can* be, the person we *long* to be, the person we truly are—through the blood of his Son.

As Paul J. Pastor so eloquently puts it:

> Creation is love, and the Creator is our Lover. God is love, and so the Spirit is love, and in creating and sustaining us, he loves us in the most specific of possible ways—numbering our hairs, maintaining the existence of our constituent molecules, manifesting his presence in every joy and grief we experience. Giving us form, being, and duration. Knowing us. Being known by us. . . .
>
> Whether you know it or not, whether you have ever felt it or heard it personally for yourself, we have all had the holy words spoken over us: *"It's good that you are; how wonderful that you exist!"*[14]

## Prayer is an invitation to worship.

Have you ever watched a movie that left you awestruck, pinned to your seat as tears and credits rolled, not wanting the feeling, the moment, to end? Longing for that noble person or deed or world to be real? Aching, you tried to hang on to a shred of that inspiration till you were wrung out from the wanting, the wishing for what could not be. Dazed, you stumbled out of the theater, blinking as the light of the sun pierced your eyes and broke the spell.

Welcome to an earthly taste of worship and awe. Humans are made to worship, and big feelers in particular love to be awed, to be rendered speechless by beauty, majesty, power, nobility.

Turn your eyes, your heart, to God, and at last you will find what true worship is meant to be. At last with God, we find one worthy of raised hands and a near-exploding heart. At last we find a hero without fault, an object of adoration without flaw. At last we find one who is real, not falsely idealized or glamorized by writers (or directors) with deceitful pens (and cameras).

David knew how to worship with every facet of his keenly emotional heart:

> Praise be to the LORD,
> > for he has heard my cry for mercy.
> The LORD is my strength and my shield;
> > my heart trusts in him, and he helps me.
> My heart leaps for joy,
> > and with my song I praise him.
>
> PSALM 28:6-7

If you've never given yourself over to worship God with the full force of your feelings, how much you have to look forward to! I urge you to cultivate a spirit of constant worship in your heart. To transform every day, every sensitive soul-moment, into an opportunity for worship, a time in which you praise, pray, and sanctify the mundane by bringing it into the presence of the Almighty.

Robert E. Webber calls this kind of worship "contemplation":

> Our *spiritual life* is the living out of God's union with
> us through contemplation and participation: the

worship of God as a style of life. . . . Contemplation is a prayerful pondering of the mystery, a wonder, a sense of astonishment and awe before the glory of it all. . . . Our contemplation . . . is a real, genuine, internal delight in the story of God's rescue of creatures and creation. This delight in God expresses itself in the worship of God translated as a love for the story, a love for life, a love for this world.[15]

We encounter opportunities for worship all day. Have you ever heard a perfect chord, an exquisite expression of musical ecstasy, and then—after looking around to make sure no one was watching—plugged in headphones and listened on repeat, turning the volume louder, ever louder, practically damaging your hearing in your desperation to grasp at the feeling, hear every note all at once, keep it ringing forever? *Own* those moments. And don't just listen—praise. Praise and thank the one who invented music, who designed the mathematics and genius behind rhythm and chords, who made our ears to hear and acoustics to amplify the sound—praise him. Turn those fleeting earthly experiences into eternal heavenly praise.

Are you beginning to see how these simple acts of worship might transform your walk with God? Can you see how they take your emotional nature—these things you see and admire and wonder over and point out somewhat sheepishly to your friends—and turn them all into a glorious life of joyful worship? You are invited into a life of constant communion with the one who made it all, the one who grins and leans in close when you praise him.

### Prayer is an invitation to enjoy.

You know those precious relationships where you just *get* each other? You understand without speaking, love without judging, relate without trying? This is the kind of relationship we are invited to cultivate with God. And with him, there's no need to rearrange calendars to achieve an hour-long coffee break when both of you are free. He is always free. Always available.

And his truths are always true. His observations are endlessly fascinating. His inventions are ever magnificent. His jokes are always funny. (Oh, yes, God has a sense of humor—he invented humor! Take a closer look at Scripture . . . and platypuses. And toddlers.)

If you've never tried to enjoy God before—if he has always been a distant giver of commands or perhaps a rigid, unapproachable object of worship—I pray you learn to enjoy him. We start enjoying him by enjoying his creation, recognizing it all as an extension of his beautiful, creative, joyful heart. We start enjoying him by reading Scripture with fresh eyes, seeking not just the intimidating and the holy, but also the joyful and the kind, the points of personal connection.

### Prayer is an invitation to share life.

This may be the most astounding of all the invitations. The Creator of the universe, Author of all things, offers to share his heart—and care about ours? Unthinkable! The Almighty invites humans to share the details of our little lives with him? Preposterous! The Alpha and Omega wants to count the ever-changing number of hairs on our insignificant heads? Ridiculous, an utter waste of his time! And yet he does. And yet he cares. To him this sharing of life and intimacy is neither preposterous nor ridiculous; it is a natural extension of his paternal love.

We see this love all throughout the Old Testament in the way God speaks of the nation of Israel:

> The LORD confides in those who fear him;
> he makes his covenant known to them.
>
> PSALM 25:14

I thought to myself,
> "I would love to treat you as my own children!"
I wanted nothing more than to give you this beautiful land—
> the finest possession in the world.
I looked forward to your calling me "Father,"
> and I wanted you never to turn from me.

JEREMIAH 3:19, NLT

And then came Jesus, who knew God more intimately than any of us ever could, and he helps us see how God loves each one of us. A father who counts hairs and gives gifts. A shepherd who leaves the ninety-nine to find the one. A protector who lifts us onto his all-bearing shoulders and carries us when our little legs grow tired.

This is our God, the God who loves us. Have you ever thought that God doesn't have time for you and all your feelings? Have you ever avoided praying because you didn't want to bother him? *God has a universe to run, plagues to manage, famines to heal, national crises to oversee, terror attacks to avert. I shouldn't bother him with my work drama, my hurt feelings, my sad child, my broken heart, my insecurities, my anxiety problem, my financial worries, my health issues . . .*

We love—and are loved by—the God who stands outside time. Omnipresent, omniscient. All loving, all powerful. God has time for you. All the time in the world and then some. He owns time; he is not bound by time.

And there are no limits to his care and concern. If it matters to you, it matters to him. Family troubles, money troubles, romance troubles—God cares about it all. He wants to hear about it all. To guide you through it, sure, but also just to listen and love and comfort as you stumble your way through.

Let's look at some examples of specific prayer from Scripture.

David, the deep-feeling psalmist, prayed about everything in his life. He prayed about:

> his friendships
> his family
> his insecurities
> his loneliness
> his heartaches and sufferings
> his victories and joys
> his thoughts and feelings
> his health
> the health of his child
> his home
> his sins
> his righteousness
> his frustration with evil and with evil people
> his disappointments
> his sleep
> his worship
> his conflicts[16]

These prayers are not recorded in the Bible by accident. God made sure they were included to instruct us and invite us. God called David a man after God's own heart, and if you and I learn to pray as David did, we, too, can echo his heart. We, too, can have intimacy with God.

### Prayer is an invitation to surrender.

Surrender is where our relationship with God differs vastly from all other relationships. With God, if we want to be close, we must surrender to his ways, his loving guidance, his for-our-own-good parameters.

You Israelites, I will judge each of you according to your own ways, declares the Sovereign LORD. Repent! Turn away from all your offenses; then sin will not be your downfall. Rid yourselves of all the offenses you have committed, and get a new heart and a new spirit.
Why will you die, people of Israel? For I take no pleasure in the death of anyone, declares the Sovereign LORD. Repent and live!

EZEKIEL 18:30-32

Have you ever worn yourself out fighting a losing battle against God? Determined to do things your own way, staying stubborn in your sin . . . and then you found your prodigal self in the muck of the pigpen, longing for home?

When we surrender our sin, our worldly ways, our worldly ambitions, to our loving Father, how quick he is to meet us on the road, to cut off our speech of apology before we're even finished, to welcome us back into close communion once more. If we want to live in God's house, we must abide by his rules—and what a relief that is! What a relief to let him be in charge. To let him set our course. To trust that he guides our steps rightly. To know that his ways always work, even when life doesn't.

## A WORD OF CAUTION ABOUT PRAYER

Let's be clear about one thing: prayer is not about conjuring a bunch of feelings. There will be some times—indeed, many times—when we pray without feeling a surge of emotion. Prayer is a practice, not a feeling—but it's a practice in which we are invited to express and experience all our feelings as needed. We are free to bring emotion into our walk with God, to be the emotional and expressive souls we are—but we don't need to feel pressure to do so constantly.

I don't wake up every morning in ecstatic raptures over my walk with God. Many days I simply show up to spend time with him out of commitment to our relationship, a habit of devotion. That commitment is important because it fosters the security and intimacy that *lead* to moments of emotional connection—but not always. Not every day. Some days you will feel as if the heavens open and angels sing in your prayer life; other days you will just talk matter-of-factly—about people, problems, and plans. That's totally fine! Prayer is our means of communication with God, and although he never changes, *we* do. Nonemotional prayer times are just as valid as emotional ones, and we need not seek constant fireworks in our walk with God.

Like all relationships, the tone of our relationship with God is subject to many variables, including our mood, stress level, and exhaustion level. We need emotional connection to keep our relationship strong, but our relationship is not *based on* or *dependent upon* those feelings. Just as a marriage is not invalid because you wake up one morning feeling *meh* about your spouse, so your relationship with God is not insincere because you go through a day or a season of days when you aren't feeling all the feels with God.

As with all relationships, our walk with God needs to be consistently nurtured. And in many ways, a habit of devotion is more important than a flood of emotion. We don't have to wait to feel like praying—or wait till we feel a certain way—in order to spend time with God.

## WORKING OUT INTENSE FEELINGS WITH GOD

One of the greatest gifts prayer gives us is a safe place to bring our intense feelings—not just to dump them (though righteous dumping is allowed), but also to work through them. To feel (and pray and reason) our way to the other side.

God has blessed me with some patient people to listen to my angsty feelings and to help me work through them, and believe me, I have poured out my junk in many a couch-soaking, hand-wringing, tissue-twisting conversation. But the trouble is, even when people help me work through a feeling, some residue remains. We may be done talking, but I'm not done feeling. I'm still twitchy—or worse. I learned long ago that I had to finish my feelings with God. People could never do for me what only God and the Spirit were meant to do.

People can't give us peace—God gives us peace.

People can't appease our consciences—God must do that.

People can't give us a change of heart—God changes hearts.

People can't forgive us when we sin against God—God forgives.

Here's what I do when I have a feeling (or feelings) I can't get rid of. First, I sit down alone with God. I tell him what's on my mind. I try to describe the feeling as specifically as I can. I usually have to write it down to really get it out properly. If I try talking or whisper-praying or praying in my head, I find I'm all over the place, rambling with no end in sight: "I feel angry because so-and-so was unfair and it brought up a million insecurities and doesn't she know that's unkind and hurts people and how could she act like that and I know Jesus doesn't want us to judge, but seriously, why do people act like that and I feel guilty because I kind of want you to punish her and that's sinful and now I feel like a horrible person and I'm sorry I know I need grace too and you won't forgive me unless I forgive her and—" You see what I mean? (Please say you've been there too.)

So I start by writing down what I'm feeling. I simplify and streamline it as much as possible:

What happened?

How did it make me feel?

What did it make me think?

What insecurity/sin/bad memory did it bring up?

What do I want God to do about this situation?

What does God want *me* to do about this situation (if anything)?

What would help me let go of this feeling?

I pray my way through it all, and many times, I write my prayer down, just like a letter. Writing prayers may be a new practice for you, but if your thoughts and feelings tend to run wild, you may find it helpful. It slows down our thoughts, directs them to one sentence at a time, and helps us stay focused on a single train of thought.

By the end of my prayer, I try to reach a resolution. This is the tricky part. I tell God, "Here is what I am asking you to do about this feeling, situation, relationship, or concern. Here's what I think you want me to do—and I'm presenting my decision and plan to you, asking you to guide me elsewhere if I'm not on the right path. Now I ask you to enable me to follow through, and I leave this [worry/fear/insecurity/problem/situation/person] with you—in your capable hands. I trust that you are aware and engaged and in control. I give this to you, God. I trust you. Please help me to feel differently soon—to feel more [peace or forgiveness or whatever it is I need to feel]. I know I may not immediately feel different, but please move me toward the right feeling. In the meantime, I choose to focus on something else while you work. I choose to act as though I feel better, trusting that you can help my feelings to follow my actions."

I still sometimes end my prayers feeling a bit funky, but I am usually calmer, more focused, and more aware of what God thinks and what he wants me to do moving forward. I feel less all over the place.

\* \* \*

A deeper walk with God will help you to live with all the feels. It will fulfill your deepest longings: the desire to know and be known, to love and be loved, to share all your inexpressible feelings with someone who—finally, truly—understands. In God you find it all. What delight he took in crafting your precious, one-of-a-kind, deep-feeling soul, and what joy he will take as you draw close to him: "Come near to God and he will come near to you" (James 4:8).

Draw near. Look no more. You've found the relationship you've always wanted.

## FEELING YOUR WAY FORWARD
### Prayer Prompt

As the deer pants for streams of water,
    so my soul pants for you, my God.
My soul thirsts for God, for the living God.
    When can I go and meet with God?

PSALM 42:1-2

How lovely is your dwelling place,
    LORD Almighty!
My soul yearns, even faints,
    for the courts of the LORD;
my heart and my flesh cry out
    for the living God.

PSALM 84:1-2

## Journal Prompts

1. How does surrendering to God's will and ways in prayer enable us to more fully experience the other aspects of our relationship with him (enjoying God's presence, worshiping, sharing life, etc.)? What do you need to surrender to God in prayer?

2. How can you share life with God each day? What would that practice look like for you? What would it feel like?

3. What do you most enjoy about God? When do you feel closest to God?

4. How do you feel about bringing your most intense emotions to God? Do you think he wants to hear them and help you resolve them? Why or why not?

# CHAPTER 13

# A BIG FEELER'S GUIDE TO THE BIBLE

You'd think the Bible would be a safe place for big feelers—a place where we always feel known. Drawn out, not shut down. And many times—maybe even most of the time—the Bible does feel like that. But then there are the other times. The times when we read the Bible and we stumble.

Maybe it's a difficult passage that reveals God's holy wrath.

Maybe it's a mind-bending passage that displays God's sovereignty.

Or maybe it's simply a hard-hitting Scripture that, to our tender natures, seems harsh. Even unfair.

Our first thought is denial: *Did the Bible just say that?* Then confusion: *Maybe I'm misreading this.* We try reading in a different translation. We feel worse.

And then comes doubt, knocking on the door of our hearts

with an unwanted delivery: a seed of insecurity. Or a root of mistrust. Or perhaps the bitter bloom of rebellion.

And then all the feelings start spiraling: *I'm a terrible Christian—no, I'm a terrible human! Did I just criticize the Bible? Or (gulp) God? Oh, I'm going to burn for this. I can't show my face at church. No one else thinks things like this. But I can't. Stop. Thinking. It. That passage is unfair! It's . . . it's unkind! It's hurtful! So either God isn't who I always thought he was, or this whole Christianity thing is a sham.*

We big feelers can get tangled up in theology more easily than most. We may hiccup over hot-button issues in Scripture, like these:

- The role of women in marriage and in church leadership: Why so specific?
- God's commands about gender and sexuality: Why so rigid?
- War and bloodshed in the Bible: Why so much killing when Jesus said turn the other cheek?
- The exclusivity of salvation: Why so narrow? Can all those other religions *really* be wrong?
- The hard sayings of Jesus: Why so intense? (News flash: Contrary to the paintings hanging in Sunday school classrooms, he wasn't all baby-holding and lamb-petting. He said some intense things. For example, there was that incident with a whip in the Temple, and another that involved some creative name calling—see Matthew 23:27.)

Or maybe for you the difficulty isn't so much with the theological complexities in Scripture; maybe your struggle is more personal. You feel pummeled and overwhelmed by every command and condemnation in the Bible, assuming each one is directed straight at you.

For all these reasons, this chapter is especially devoted to helping big feelers in their relationship with Scripture. But don't get me wrong—although big feelers may be the most prone to doubt, they aren't the only ones who wrestle with their faith. I know many a steady feeler or reluctant feeler who gets tangled up in questions and qualms. If you have ever faced difficulties in your faith or Bible reading, the principles and practical tips in this chapter may help you too.

I've found that doubt generally falls into one of two categories: theological or personal. Theological doubt has to do with the overarching tough questions of faith: the wrath of God, the sovereignty of God, the reasons for suffering. Personal doubt has to do with God's involvement in your life: *Does God love me? Am I forgiven? Does this difficulty in my life mean I'm being punished by God?*

So what's a doubter to do?

Our goal in this chapter is to acknowledge the faith difficulties faced by deep feelers who also think deeply. We're not going to tackle the Hard Questions in the Bible, because that's a different book altogether, and many theologians with multiple initials behind their names have already done a bang-up job on that count.

So let's talk about how God treats doubters and then explore some practical tips for deep feelers as we read the Bible and wrestle with doubt.

## FRUSTRATED OR FASCINATED?

When I read the Bible, an unbidden voice often pops up in my mind, asking annoyingly direct and occasionally combative questions:

*But why?*

*Says who?*

*How is that fair?*

For a long time I felt guilty for being this way. Why didn't faith come as easily to me as it seems to for other people? Why was I always studying some issue or doctrine that bothered me while everybody else was just singing "Amazing Grace" and basking in the love of God?

Every time a new question or doubt sprang up, I'd panic: *Oh no! I'm doubting again.* And if I couldn't quickly find a satisfactory resolution for my question, I decided the whole Bible-God-Jesus thing must be a hoax. I was sure everything would crumble! (And there you have another lovely example of Worst-Case Scenario Disorder with an added dose of Panic Mode.)

I've learned to ease up on the self-guilt. I've learned to (mostly) avoid Panic Mode. I've learned that instead of feeling frustrated— *Why isn't this issue clear in Scripture? Why do I have so many pesky questions? Why can't I just accept and believe?*—I need to let my questions fascinate me.

Being fascinated means you lean into the questions instead of running from them. It means you embrace the questioning part of yourself as an integral part of your character, your faith, and the way you relate to God. It means you understand that God made you a deep thinker and that he will work *with you* as you deepen your faith. As you draw near to God—asking questions, studying, thinking, and praying—God will draw near to you.

I truly believe that our faith will be stronger if we wrestle through it than if we accept everything without study or thought. Our faith will be more complex and nuanced because of our questions. And believe it or not, our doubts can also help others.

If faith doesn't come easily for you; if you have more questions about God, Jesus, and the Bible than you wish you had; if you sometimes wish you could shut off the cross-examiner who lives inside you against your will, welcome to the deep-feeling, deep-thinking club. Join the rest of us who cry, alongside the man who needed Jesus to heal his son, "I do believe! But also help me overcome my unbelief!" (see Mark 9:24).

## TWO DOUBTERS, TWO RESPONSES

Before we move on to practical thoughts on reading Scripture, let's do a little case study about how God treated two doubters. Through the lives of Gideon and Zechariah, the Bible gives us fascinating examples of how God "parented" two of his children through their expressions of doubt.

Gideon was visited by an angel, who announced, "The LORD is with you, mighty warrior" (Judges 6:12). Gideon hemmed and hawed for a while, insecure and unconvinced, but finally decided the angel must be serious and he should probably rise to the challenge. He did the first thing the angel asked (in the dark, under cover of night, but still—he did it). He called an army to himself, and the Israelites rallied around him. But then, as the danger grew more intense, Gideon got nervous. The story goes like this:

> Gideon said to God, "If you will save Israel by my hand as you have promised—look, I will place a wool fleece on the threshing floor. If there is dew only on the fleece and all the ground is dry, then I will know that you will save Israel by my hand, as you said." And that is what happened. Gideon rose early the next day; he squeezed the fleece and wrung out the dew—a bowlful of water.
> JUDGES 6:36-38

Gideon needed encouragement—he yearned to believe, he longed to be brave—and he asked God for a sign proving his presence and faithfulness. And God did it! But the story isn't over. Doubt was still knocking at Gideon's heart, whispering through the keyhole—*Maybe it was a coincidence!*—so Gideon asked for a second sign:

Then Gideon said to God, "Do not be angry with me. Let me make just one more request. Allow me one more test with the fleece, but this time make the fleece dry and let the ground be covered with dew."

JUDGES 6:39

Did God zap Gideon with lightning and choose someone else—someone braver, someone quicker to believe? No—God gave Gideon a second miracle:

That night God did so. Only the fleece was dry; all the ground was covered with dew.

JUDGES 6:40

Isn't that amazing? God's grace and patience on beautiful display.

Now let's time-travel forward about 1,100 years to meet a priest named Zechariah. Poor Zechariah didn't enjoy the same gentle parenting Gideon received. Zechariah and his wife, Elizabeth, were righteous but barren, and they were older—most likely in their sixties or beyond. Not only had their parenting window closed, their *life* window was closing too.

One once-in-a-lifetime day, Zechariah was chosen to enter the Holy of Holies to make the sin offering. (This was an honor a priest might receive only once in his life—if ever.) While he was ministering behind the curtain, the angel Gabriel appeared and said: "Do not be afraid, Zechariah; your prayer has been heard. Your wife Elizabeth will bear you a son, and you are to call him John. . . . He will . . . make ready a people prepared for the Lord" (Luke 1:13-14, 17).

And then Zechariah fell to his knees in worship and thanks— oh, wait. No, he didn't. Let's just say this wasn't Zechariah's shining moment of faith. I picture the scene unfolding something like this:

Zechariah blinks for a long moment, then stammers, "How can I be sure of this? I am an old man and my wife is well along in years."

One of Gabriel's eyebrows rockets up. "I am Gabriel." He seems to grow larger, and the room grows dimmer even as his skin takes on an iridescent glow. Zechariah shrinks into a corner, trembling.

Gabriel continues, "I stand in the presence of God, and I have been sent to speak to you and to tell you this good news. And now you will be silent and not able to speak until the day this happens, because you did not believe my words, which will come true at their appointed time."

Thunder cracks, and a roar builds, filling the room, Zechariah's head, and the Holy of Holies. Zechariah's ears ring and then buzz, until . . . nothing. No sound remains.

Zechariah opens his mouth to apologize, to take it back, to beg forgiveness, to proclaim faith, but his throat swallows his voice. His hands flutter to his throat.

He blinks as he looks around the room, but Gabriel is gone. Zechariah is alone with his regret and his news. *His news!* He claps a hand to his mouth, wishing he could shout, laugh, cry—oh, to see Elizabeth's shocked expression when she understands! Oh, the joy that will light her face when her aging arms hold a son at last . . .

He falls to his knees in prayer—contrition, humility, gratitude. Tears wet his cheeks as his mouth shapes words without sound.*

Two angelic encounters, two doubting men—two dramatically different responses from God. So what can we take from this? I suggest that God treats us as individuals. He searches our hearts,

---

* See Luke 1:5-25. Note that the dialogue is taken word for word from the NIV.

knows our hearts—time and again the Bible repeats this refrain\*—
and he, loving and wise Father, parents us accordingly.

We might consider a few differences between the two men.
Gideon was a farmer, a man who had lived seven years under
Midian's harsh rule, and he no doubt felt defeated and discouraged. Neither prince nor priest, Gideon held no special title
that we know of. Zechariah, in contrast, was a priest from the line
of Aaron. He'd been raised with the best spiritual training, the
most access to God. Perhaps for these reasons, God's expectations
were a bit higher for him. He was also an older man, while Gideon
was younger—we don't know how young, but young enough that
his own father was still alive. Perhaps (and, of course, this is specu-
lation) God made allowances for Gideon's age and inexperience.

Regardless of the reasons God treated these two doubters
differently, the fact remains: God treated them differently. And
therein lies the help we need. Even when we struggle with doubt,
we can come confidently to God, knowing that just as he searched
the hearts of these men, so he searches ours. And you and I have
an advantage even these two great men lacked: we have Jesus at
the right hand of God, speaking on our behalf:

> Who will bring any charge against those whom God
> has chosen? It is God who justifies. Who then is the one
> who condemns? No one. Christ Jesus who died—more
> than that, who was raised to life—is at the right hand of
> God and is also interceding for us.
>
> ROMANS 8:33-34

---

\* See Psalm 139:23; Jeremiah 17:10; Romans 8:27; Revelation 2:23.

## SCRIPTURE-READING SUGGESTIONS

Let's begin by establishing some helpful guidelines for reading Scripture:

### 1. Don't over-identify or over-personalize.

God's specific instructions or comments to a particular person or group of people in Scripture thousands of years ago don't always reflect the way he relates to or deals with his people today—and they don't always necessarily reflect his relationship with *you*. Sometimes they do, but not always. Sometimes God made comments, delivered judgments, and mandated behaviors intended for a specific person or group of people, and those words do not *directly* apply to us today in the same way. That doesn't mean we can't learn from God's words to past people, but we may not always be able to apply them directly to our own circumstances.

For example, in Mark 10, Jesus encounters a wealthy young man who is eager to please God. He falls at Jesus' feet and says, "Good teacher, what must I do to be saved?" After a brief exchange, Jesus looks at the man, feels a surge of affection for him, and says, "One thing you lack. Go, sell everything you have and give to the poor, and you will have treasure in heaven. Then come, follow me" (Mark 10:21). The man walks away sad, unwilling to give up his earthly riches in exchange for heavenly treasure. This conversation cuts first-world modern readers to the quick, does it not? We read it, we feel a challenge to our own comfort and materialism, and we can't help but wonder, *Would I have walked away sad too?* And those uncomfortable emotions—awareness, self-analysis, conviction—are not bad things to feel. But do we then need to take Jesus' challenge to this young man as a command we also must obey—or as a command every Christian must obey? To truly please God, do we all need to sell everything we own and give it to the poor? Is it inherently sinful to own property or possessions as a follower of Christ? The answer to both questions is, of course, no.

Although Jesus often spoke about greed and called his followers to hold lightly to their earthly loves—and we should take those exhortations to heart—he did not call every disciple to sell everything they owned. He gave the sell-everything command only one time, to this one man. Jesus looked into the rich ruler's heart, identified the one thing standing in the way of his wholehearted devotion to God, and challenged it. Now, even though you and I don't necessarily need to have a garage sale—and then sell the garage—in order to follow Jesus, that doesn't mean we can't learn from this conversation. This passage is a sobering reminder of the power of greed, the pull of the world, and the temptation to put other things before God. It is a humbling reminder that Jesus must come first, and we must rid our hearts of all idols. It is an inspiring reminder of Jesus' love for the poor—a love he wants us to wholly embrace in both emotional and practical ways. This passage helps us understand how we can learn from Scripture even if it applies somewhat differently to us than it did to its initial audience.

Take a step back and think like a parent for a moment. Most parents have general household rules that apply to everyone in the home, but wise parents deal with each of their children as individuals, according to their needs and personalities and unique circumstances. Some kids are easily won over and brought to repentance when they make mistakes; others need a bit more—uh, "convincing." One of my kids was so softhearted as a toddler that I barely had to look at him sideways to get him to dissolve into a puddle of repentant tears; another was so—er, we'll call it "determined"—that we had many epic confrontations (most famously the Great Princess Dress Showdown, when I marched into her closet, pulled out all the princess dresses, and relocated them to my closet, where they hung, alone in their glittery splendor, until she earned them back one by one). Different kids, different hearts, different kinds of discipline.

Every Scripture you read will not apply directly to you every time you read it. Let me clarify: every Scripture was written for a reason and should be read and digested with reverence and respect. But depending on where you are in life and what issues and temptations you are currently dealing with, different Scriptures will apply differently at different times. Some may never resonate on a deep personal level. (For example, although some of us may never feel personally convicted by the Scriptures that say, "Do not steal," most of us will relate to admonitions about coveting and envy.)

For many years, in an effort to be submissive to God's Word, I tried to glean some deep personal lesson from every passage I read every time I read it, but over time I came to realize I was wearing myself out spiritually, banging myself over the head with Scriptures that didn't address my current spiritual condition. My friend, if the scriptural shoe doesn't fit, don't jam it on your foot and wear it around town all day. You'll end up with bloodied toes and shin splints!

## 2. Assume the best, not the worst.

For many years, when I encountered a difficult passage, the catastrophizer in me would take over, Worst-Case-Scenario Disorder would kick in, and I'd jump to the most desperate conclusion, something like *Grace is a false hope! God hates people! We are all DOOMED!* Even after all my years basking in the grace and love of God, having experienced his kindness time and again, a single confusing Scripture could set me reeling.

But I'm growing. I'm learning to take a step back, take a deep breath (or twenty), and rearrange my thoughts. I'm trying to start from a place of trust rather than doubt. To remind myself of the million reassuring things I *know* to be true about God, his Word, and his ways . . . and then start from there—that faithful place—as I grapple with the tricky passage. That simple realignment changes everything.

### 3. Don't panic.

See number two.

But seriously, don't panic over finding a Scripture that's tough to understand. Though humans served as scribes, the Bible was ultimately written by the Almighty God. By the God who said, "My ways [are] higher than your ways and my thoughts than your thoughts" (Isaiah 55:9). Of course we don't understand everything he says and does. If we did, *we* would be God!

I have finally realized that difficult passages can either frustrate me or fuel my study. When I encounter a passage that stumps me, I can either run from it or lean into it by studying it, researching it, and seeking godly counsel from wise people who know their Bibles.

### 4. Don't shut down. Keep thinking; keep studying.

We all have triggers—issues that, when pushed, hit some deep-down place of conviction or pain or insecurity. Maybe they are issues from our childhood or temptations we've struggled to overcome or causes we feel personally passionate about. And sometimes the Bible brushes up against those triggers. When that happens, we have a choice. We can shut down or dive deep.

I choose to dive deep. I refuse to throw my faith out the window every time I encounter a passage or principle that makes me uncomfortable. Instead, I choose to ask questions, study more, pray harder. It's not the easiest route, but the payoff is worth it.

## 5. Don't read selectively.

If you're a deep thinker, you can't be a selective Bible reader. It's not going to work for you. You can't just play "Bible roulette" every morning: *What do I want to read today?* [Spin Bible, open at random, point finger at passage, read.] We all do that on occasion, but if you have a more sensitive understanding of faith, you won't thrive on a steady diet of random reading. You can't do casual drop-ins on difficult passages without taking time to learn a bit about the context and culture. I promise I'm not trying to over-whelm you here—please don't panic and shut down. (See points 2 and 3.) I'm not suggesting you go get a Bible degree, only that you commit to a more focused and intentional style of Bible study that sets you up for faith and growth.

With that in mind, you'll notice I quote a lot of Scriptures in this book. My hope is that by the time you get to the end, you will have assembled a stockpile of Scriptures to cling to as you move forward in your faith. I also offer several free downloads and articles on my website, ElizabethLaingThompson.com, to help you apply Scripture to specific emotions.

## 6. Don't modernize the Bible.

Because they had different perspectives and cultural influences, ancient people thought differently than we do—about God, science, nature, family, slavery, diet, marriage roles, community expectations, and a host of other issues. And just as he does with us, God met them where they were. This means he sometimes made laws or even allowances that made sense for their lifestyle and perspective.

For example, for many years I was troubled by Numbers 5, where God gave Moses strange instructions for what to do when a jealous husband accused his wife of adultery. I thought, *How unjust! What a horrible way to treat women!* And then I read a commentary that enlightened me: this practice was given for the *protection* of women. In most ancient societies (with Judaism as a blessed exception), women were viewed as little more than property. Even in Jewish society, an unfounded accusation by a paranoid husband could send a helpless woman out on the streets with no honor, no money, and no way of making a living. So even though the method itself sounds bizarre to the modern ear, it was actually God's grace and concern for women in action.

## 7. Beware "good kid in a bad class" syndrome.

When my mom, Geri, was in first grade, she came home in tears, wailing, "I'm terrible! I'm always in trouble in school!" Concerned, my grandmother arranged a meeting with her teacher. When Grandma asked what my mom was doing to get in so much trouble, the baffled teacher replied, "What are you talking about? Geri is wonderful! She always listens, always does exactly what I say." My grandmother realized that every time the teacher corrected the class as a group, my sweet mother had been internalizing the rebuke as her own. In Mom's mind, the class wasn't being bad—*she* was being bad.

Several years ago, I had one of those head-spinning *aha* moments about the Bible. I read a particularly scathing rebuke to the Israelites. I can't remember which one—probably something from early Isaiah—and I got a pit in my stomach. Dutifully, I attempted to apply the rebuke to my own current spirituality, even though it felt strained. And in that moment I realized, *No wonder this feels forced! It's because this Scripture is not speaking to me. At least not to where I am spiritually right now.*

A light dawned. My head buzzed. Angels sang. (Not really, but you know the feeling.) It was like being set free after decades of self-imposed, unnecessary misery and bondage.

I learned a powerful lesson that day: I don't ever want to be hardhearted or blind to my own weakness, but neither do I want to take on other people's sins. I always want to remain open to God's discipline, to seeing ways I can grow and change, but I don't need to take on every hard-hitting passage as a personal reproach meant just for me. If I'm not struggling with, say, idol worship or sexual immorality, I need not flog myself into sorrow and repentance when I read a scathing passage on the topic. I can read it, say to myself, *Wow, that's good motivation for never going there in my heart,* and then . . . I can move on. Have a happy day. Run free in the grace and love of God.

Are there times when I sin and need the Bible's hard passages to set me straight? Of course. But if the whole-class rebuke isn't intended for me, I don't need to put myself in some kind of self-imposed torment. And God wouldn't want me to do so.

My daughter and I both wear glasses: she because she is near-sighted; I because the number of birthdays I've celebrated seems to have adversely affected my vision, and I now need reading glasses to see small print. Cassidy recently got a new pair of glasses, and out of curiosity, I put them on. The whole world went blurry. My eyes began to throb. But wait—does that mean my daughter's glasses have the wrong prescription? Are Cassidy's glasses faulty or invalid because they don't help everyone who puts them on to see more clearly? Of course not! Cassidy's glasses have the perfect prescription . . . for *her* eyes.

You aren't being prideful if you say, "Hmm, what a fabulous passage . . . for someone else. Maybe one day I will relate to it more, but not today." God wrote the Bible with many different spiritual prescriptions in mind, addressing every conceivable temptation, sin, and personality type. Don't borrow other people's prescriptions, my sensitive friend. If a hard-hitting Scripture doesn't address the current condition of your heart, don't give yourself a headache trying to make it fit. Read it, respectfully acknowledge its intrinsic value and wisdom, and move on to a passage that does apply to you.

\* \* \*

The Bible is the richest book in the world. It depicts the plight of humanity with compassion, honesty, heartache, and even humor. It doesn't dodge the hard questions. It doesn't gloss over the seeming randomness of suffering or the anguish of loss. The Bible makes sense of the world, brings hope to despair, and shines light in the dark. Though you may have to fight through some questions and difficulties in your faith, I pray you put the effort in, and even enjoy the adventure of learning and growing. It's—well, it's fascinating.

## FEELING YOUR WAY FORWARD

### Prayer Prompt

> LORD, my heart is not proud;
>     my eyes are not haughty.
> I don't concern myself with matters too great
>     or too awesome for me to grasp.
> Instead, I have calmed and quieted myself,
>     like a weaned child who no longer cries for its mother's
>         milk.
>     Yes, like a weaned child is my soul within me.
> O Israel, put your hope in the LORD—
>     now and always.

PSALM 131, NLT

## Journal Prompts

1. Which type of doubt do you most struggle with: theological or personal? Why?

2. How do you feel about yourself when you doubt? How do you think God feels about you?

3. How does it feel to realize that many godly people in Scripture wrestled with doubt? How does that realization change your perspective on your own questions?

4. What questions do you have about your faith? Where might you begin in your Bible study to address those issues? If you aren't sure where to start, what friends, advisers, or other resources could you approach for guidance?

# CHAPTER 14

# HARNESSING EMOTIONS IN RELATIONSHIPS

Ruth watches as Orpah weeps in their mother-in-law's arms. "I—can't—bear—leaving—you." A sob between each word.

"But leave you must," Naomi says, stroking Orpah's hair as mothers do when consoling small daughters. "I have nothing to offer you anymore, my child." Her voice has that distant quality Ruth has come to hate, as if Naomi's feelings—and perhaps her compassion—died with her husband and sons, replaced by a relentless logic. As if she will acknowledge only facts from here to the grave.

"I have no home, no money, no sons," Naomi continues. "Even if I thought there was still hope for me—even if I had a husband tonight and then gave birth to sons to replace the ones you both married, would you wait for them to grow up? It is more bitter for me than for you, because the Lord's hand has gone out against me!"

Orpah lets out a muffled wail into Naomi's shoulder. Naomi's expression stays wooden.

"There now." A few awkward pats on the back. "Enough. Go back to your father's house." Naomi pushes Orpah back to arm's length, takes her daughter-in-law's quivering chin in her mottled hand. "You are young enough and pretty enough that you will find another husband. Perhaps one who likes your cooking, eh?" She grimaces—almost a smile—and Ruth knows she meant to make a joke, though it came out rather unkind.

One last, long embrace, followed by a multitude of kisses, and Orpah climbs onto the trader's wagon bound for Moab and home.

"Your turn," Naomi says, blinking fast as she faces Ruth.

But Ruth shakes her head. "Don't ask me to leave you."

Naomi bites her lip. Ruth thinks she sees it tremble. "Not you, too," Naomi says, her voice tight. "I count on you to understand. You heard what I said to Orpah. I have nothing; I am going home to my people a beggar, a burden. I cannot provide—"

Ruth turns and nods over her shoulder to the trader in the wagon behind her, the signal they had arranged when Naomi wasn't looking. He nods back and flicks the reins, and the wagon trundles away.

"Wait! Stop!" shouts Naomi. "Ruth, hurry—you must climb aboard."

The wagon does not stop. Ruth clasps Naomi's bony wrists in her hands. Naomi tries to tug free, shouts again at the wagon, but Ruth holds tight. Dust coils around their ankles. "Where you go I will go, and where you stay I will stay," she says, her voice strong but clogged with fierce affection. "Your people, my people; your God, my God. Where you die I will die, and there I will be buried."

Naomi opens her mouth, then clamps it shut. She blinks fast through red eyes. "Oh, daughter," she says, "what a foolish girl you are." But she squeezes Ruth's hands in hers, and Ruth hears the unspoken words there. The gratitude.

Naomi lets go, squares her age-crooked shoulders, and says, "Well, then. Let's find a trader heading toward Bethlehem. It's time to go home."*

Here we have the friendship that gives us one of the most poignant expressions of devotion recorded in Scripture—perhaps anywhere. The promise that launched ten million wedding vows.

Although we can't say for sure which type of feeler Ruth and Naomi were, both women were capable of intense passion, expression, and loyalty. At the beginning of the book of Ruth, we see that Naomi's heartbreak and bitterness have changed her—warped her. Convinced that God is against her (and can you blame her?), she doubts him, doubts his love, doubts herself. She loses herself for a time, even changing her name from Naomi (meaning "sweet") to Mara (meaning "bitter"). And Ruth loves her in spite of it. Loves her through it.

Naomi and Ruth's relationship captures some of what deep feelers can experience in relationships: mutual joy, lifelong devotion, relentless compassion. Ruth's commitment to her mother-in-law reflects so much of the way sensitive souls love: loyalty beyond reason, devotion past what is practical, supreme self-sacrifice, the willingness to stay when others would leave. In all this we reflect the heart of God—the way he loves us even when we are unlovable.

In this chapter, we'll take a look at the opportunities our natures open up for us relationally, along with the potential difficulties we may face. We will take a closer look at how sensitivity can affect

---

* You can find the biblical account in Ruth 1.

relationships, keeping in mind that while big feelers may be the most sensitive, steady and reluctant feelers also have tender places that need tending. But before we dive into human relationships, let's remember: people can never take the place of our relationship with God. Even in the most intimate and delightful of relationships, there will be an empty place, a this-isn't-how-it-should-be place. Here in this fallen world with our fallen hearts, that place—that feeling—will linger. Only when we're with God in heaven will that place be filled entirely.

## THE PROBLEM WITH PEOPLE

> Each heart knows its own bitterness,
>     and no one else can share its joy.
> PROVERBS 14:10

This proverb has saved my relationships and peace of mind more times than I can count. I came across it in my late teens, and the moment I read it, a bell of truth rang inside: *This is why I often feel alone!*

I had already spent my young life trying to cram my expansive feelings into the confines of words, and as much as people (ahem, thank you, Mom and Dad—you are saints) had tried to mourn or rejoice with me, tried to understand the height of my joy or the depth of my heartbreak, they couldn't. No one can step inside another person's heart and fully feel all they do.

This proverb helped me accept a hard truth: as a stubborn idealist who holds relationships to high (translation: perfect) standards, I am bound to be disappointed sometimes here on earth. I'm destined to be disappointed in myself: *Why can't I express what I feel when I feel it—and as deeply as I feel it? Why do I say too much and make people uncomfortable? Why do I get hurt too quickly?* And

I am bound to be disappointed by others: *Why doesn't anyone care as much as I need them to? Why doesn't anyone "get" this feeling—or me? Why is everyone always too busy? Why can't relationships be like the ones in books and movies?*

Here in the real world, time and distance keep us from one another. *Life* keeps us from one another. We long to connect with loved ones, but instead we have school, work, family, illness, responsibilities. We have flaws—hurtful ones. We carry baggage that baffles people, holds them at a distance, or pushes them away. We sin against one another, sometimes knowingly, often unintentionally. We fail to interpret expectations. We aren't enough to fill the hole in another person's heart.

When Kevin finally—finally! as in, two-plus years into our it-was-never-just-friendship-to-me "friendship"!—got the heavenly memo that I was the woman of his dreams, I was so ecstatic that my knock-off Doc Martens hardly touched ground for a month. He was all I could think about, all I wanted to talk about. I wanted to share with my friends every adorable nuance of every heart-melting moment we shared. And at first I tried, but I quickly realized that even the people who cared about me most got a glazed-over look after a while. Much as they shared my joy—truly, they did—they had limits. Not to mention needs and joys of their own.

But you know who had all the time in the world to listen, to celebrate, to care? *God.* I started turning to him to share all the little moments, started praying (and giving thanks!) every time my singing heart needed an outlet for all that dazzling joy. And God—ever available, ever interested, ever concerned—became the container, even the amplifier, for all that joy. I wasn't alone in my celebration anymore.

And then, a few years later, on the other end of the emotional spectrum, I went through the anguish of infertility. It was a constant onslaught of heartache: the pain, not just of today's loss, but the loss of all our tomorrows, all we had dreamed about and hoped for, the life we'd assumed we'd have when we said "I do." And so much fear: *I will never nurse a baby, never wave goodbye on the first day of kindergarten, never comfort a teenage heartbreak, never be the mother of the bride, never give grandchildren a sugar high before sending them home . . . and I will die alone.*

I shared many of these feelings with Kevin and with a set of devoted friends and family who were as sensitive and all-absorbing as they could be, but even so, no one could live every minute of the pain with me. And honestly? I was mourning so intensely, so constantly, I feared I might drag my would-be rescuers into sorrow's bog and drown them with me.

Again I learned to turn to God, this time with my heartache. He alone could handle the pain—every second of every agony. He alone could be present every time the world hammered fresh blows into my heart, hour by hour. My grief couldn't drown God; my doubts couldn't damage his faith. He could take it—he *wanted* to take it, *invited* me to hand it over (see 1 Peter 5:7)—and so I gave it to him. Poured it all into his capable hands and let him draw me close.

Now whenever I think of that proverb, I think of it like this:

> Each heart knows its own bitterness
> and no one else can share its joy . . .
> *no one, that is, but God.*

## ON LOVE AND COURAGE

Close relationships take courage. Ruth took a costly gamble that day when she refused to leave Naomi. In her bitterness, Naomi could have turned Ruth away, despising her gift. And even after Ruth had given up her own home and family to be with her mother-in-law, Naomi could have remained bitter for the rest of her life. Ruth certainly didn't throw in her lot with Naomi thinking, *I bet Naomi will eventually snap out of her grief and help me marry a great guy and give me a second chance at having a family.* No, Ruth had no guarantees—she had only love. And she gave it freely, without strings and without knowing the ending.

Because big feelers love so passionately and vulnerably, relationships can feel scary for us, risky—perhaps scarier and riskier than they do for others. Because we love so generously, so intensely, we experience a corresponding level of loss and betrayal if a relationship goes wrong. But the opposite also holds true: because we love so generously, so intensely, we experience a corresponding level of joy and fulfillment when a relationship goes well. And in the end, the reward outweighs the risk.

Vulnerability is also especially intimidating for reluctant feelers, who prefer to hold their cards close. When they do take a brave step forward in a relationship—sharing a confidence, expressing heartfelt affection, letting someone deep inside—they risk rejection or misunderstanding. That's a terrifying place to be for people who prefer not to feel emotionally compromised! But again, the reward outweighs the risk.

The key here for all feeling types is to follow the example of Jesus, who loved intensely but didn't seek his identity or confidence in people. The same Jesus who looked at people and loved them, whose heart went out to people who were hurting, did not entrust himself to those people. He loved them, gave to them, even enjoyed them, but his confidence came from God.

> While [Jesus] was in Jerusalem at the Passover Festival, many people saw the signs he was performing and believed in his name. But Jesus would not entrust himself to them, for he knew all people. He did not need any testimony about mankind, for he knew what was in each person.
>
> JOHN 2:23-25

If you've been hurt before and now you are hiding at home, barricading your heart, I hope you'll open the door to let other people inside. Look around, find some potential relationships, and when the time is right, start opening up: a little bit here, a little bit there. If we can keep in mind that God is the ultimate source of our joy and identity, then it's not such a risk to offer our hearts to fellow fallen humans. We won't be shocked if they fall, shattered if they fail. Hurt, yes, but not so hurt that we never love again.

What a sad place the world would be without your particular brand of feeling, your special way of loving and giving. The world needs you. The people in your life need you. (If you need more reminders of the particular gifts you have to offer, take a look back at chapter 2!) Without pressuring ourselves to be perfect, to take the place of God, we can offer our gifts to encourage, comfort, and strengthen others. We can give as Jesus gave—selflessly, sacrificially, without strings or expectations—knowing that somehow God returns our gifts to us:

> Give, and it will be given to you. A good measure, pressed down, shaken together and running over, will be poured into your lap. For with the measure you use, it will be measured to you.
>
> LUKE 6:38

## WHEN SENSITIVITY BACKFIRES

Let's take a closer look at how sensitivity affects relationships. We have already seen some of the strengths sensitive souls like Ruth have to offer: empathy, insight, patience, listening, devotion, generosity, self-sacrifice—reflections of Christ, each one. But as much as having a sensitive nature enhances a person's ability to experience close relationships, every strength has a shadow side, an inversion.

What are some of the trickier aspects of sensitivity? What might big-feeling types need to guard against in our relationships?

Here I've compiled a list of not-so-pleasant roles we can fall into as sensitive souls. I have fit each of these descriptions at different times—sometimes all of them all at once!

## The Insecure Soul

Big feelers notice nuance, read vibes across the room, and sense emotional shifts . . . and sometimes these insights turn inward and backfire on us. We become overly aware of people's every reaction to us, and it makes us self-conscious. And while insecurity may reach more acute levels for big feelers, steady and reluctant feelers have their share of insecure moments too.

What can help us overcome insecurity? First, we must remember a simple truth: people—even the best of people—are an unreliable source of our self-esteem. Only God is unchanging. Only God's love never fails. Only God can be the source of our security, our identity, our confidence.

Early in Jesus' ministry, when he was getting attention and fame, he guarded his heart: "I do not accept glory from human beings," he told the crowds (John 5:41).

We also have to be careful not to view every emotional shift through a personal lens. One evening my friend and I were hanging out, having a grand old time swapping stories and sharing chocolate, when her husband came home from work. After she greeted him and he left the room, her demeanor changed. She closed down, an open book slammed shut. My mind raced: *What did I say wrong? Did I ask a question I shouldn't have? Did I share something that made her uncomfortable?* Hours later I realized: her shutdown had nothing to do with me. She had smelled alcohol on her husband's breath, and she was worried about him. I'd been feeling insecure for nothing; in fact, my self-focus had made me blind to my friend's concern.

## The Angry Soul

Because big feelers feel deeply and love fiercely, we may be easily wounded by the people we love most. We make ourselves vulnerable, and the greater the vulnerability, the greater the potential for hurt. The wider the opening in our hearts, the deeper the sword can pierce.

Anger often has to do with unmet expectations. And big feelers aren't the only ones who feel disappointed by other people; everyone experiences this kind of hurt from time to time. For example, a friend doesn't call us back right away and we think, *They should call me back today. I always call them back right away.* Hurt and anger follow. Or we get sick and no one checks on us, let alone sends a card or a meal. We think, *They should at least call! If they were sick, I would check on them every day and make them chicken noodle soup! And now I'm completely alone; nobody loves me.* Our sense of justice insists, *But I would never treat someone that way! I treat others (mostly) the way I would want to be treated! They should do the same for me! Jesus said so!* We expect the golden rule to go both ways, but it doesn't always.

But it's not fair to expect others to adhere to the same code of behavior we have privately established for ourselves. Although everyone makes mistakes, most of the time other people are acting the way they think they should. Who are we to impose our definition of politeness or friendship on them?* Certainly, as Christians, we should follow Jesus' code of ethics, but we all interpret and apply it a bit differently. And that's okay!

## The Wounded Soul

Many sensitive souls carry wounds from being misunderstood in childhood—perhaps by parents, siblings, friends, teachers, or

---

* In *Feeling Good*, David Burns identifies ten cognitive distortions that lead to depression, one of which is "should" statements.

mentors. By people we needed and admired who just didn't "get" us. Maybe they treated us roughly when we needed kindness, told us to suck it up when we needed a listening ear or a comforting hug. Maybe they labeled us weird when we needed to hear, "You're normal. And you're going to be okay. God loves you and likes you no matter what—and so do I."

As young people, we didn't have the vocabulary to explain, "This is how I work, what I feel, what I need." Perhaps you are still finding those words now. Still defining your feelings, processing the hurts. When you do, it can be overwhelming to process.

Those old wounds are valid, real—and they need tending. If we're not careful, they can turn septic, sending their toxicity throughout our bodies, killing us cell by cell. Poisoning even the formerly healthy parts of our hearts. Affecting the way we relate to all future relationships, making us guarded, defensive, jaded, hard edged.

I urge you to do the heart work needed to resolve past wounds the best you can. Even if resolution is impossible face-to-face, seek forgiveness and release in prayer and in your own heart. Decide not to let your past taint your future. You may not be able to go back in time to correct those old relationships, and you can't control how other people relate to you, but you can decide how—and who—you want to be in your relationships moving forward.

## The Easily Offended Soul

Sometimes the things that hurt us aren't deep wounds; they're smaller injuries. Our sensitivity can make us . . . well, sensitive. Easily hurt by harsh tones of voice, small slights, thoughtless acts of unkindness. I'm not saying these injuries are illegitimate, but we big-feeling types may be more aware of them than other people are—and more deeply affected by them. I won't say, "Don't be so sensitive" (because we all know how helpful *that* is!), but I will say,

"Be wise (intentional, thoughtful) about when and how often and to whom you *express* your sensitivity."

When I'm tempted to be easily offended, I find that the best defense is a good offense. Instead of focusing on how others are treating me and loving me, I focus on how I am treating and loving them. I decide to think about what I can *give* instead of what I wish I were receiving. The more selfless we are in our relationships, the less we'll get hung up on hurt feelings and unmet expectations.

Our role model in this is, of course, Jesus. Jesus, the Word of God, through whom all things were created. Jesus, the honorable man who never got the honor he deserved. Jesus, the compassionate servant who didn't receive the kind of love he so generously gave. Jesus, the friend of all, who was often misunderstood and let down by his friends. Jesus, the Lamb of God, who was abused, betrayed, and left to bleed alone in his hour of greatest need:

> He grew up before him like a tender shoot,
> and like a root out of dry ground.
> He had no beauty or majesty to attract us to him,
> nothing in his appearance that we should
> desire him.
> He was despised and rejected by mankind,
> a man of suffering, and familiar with pain.
> Like one from whom people hide their faces
> he was despised, and we held him in low esteem.
>
> Surely he took up our pain
> and bore our suffering,
> yet we considered him punished by God,
> stricken by him, and afflicted.

But he was pierced for our transgressions,
    he was crushed for our iniquities;
the punishment that brought us peace was on him,
    and by his wounds we are healed.

ISAIAH 53:2-5

When we remember Jesus—how much he suffered, how much he forgave—our small injuries fade in comparison. In light of Jesus' light, we can let go of the little things.

## The Always-about-Me Soul

Capable as big feelers are of intense devotion and selfless sacrifice, sometimes we don't fulfill those capabilities. Sometimes our own emotions become so overpowering they are all we can feel, all we can see. They dominate our thoughts, our conversations, our relationships. This is particularly true when we go through a season of heightened anxiety or sadness. Our own feelings become all consuming, and we struggle to see beyond our own emotional borders to what others need.

When we finally find a safe person who understands us, we feel free—perhaps for the first time in a long time, or ever—to open up and unload. And that's fine—in fact, it's a wonderful gift! But let's not forget to reciprocate. Relationships must go two ways.

For steady feelers and reluctant feelers, your "always-about-me" moments may happen unintentionally when you are unaware of others' feelings. You're hanging out, you're having a good time . . . but you don't realize your bigger-feeling friend needs to talk about something. Because you don't personally relate to being frequently overwhelmed by emotion, you may need to remind yourself that the big feelers in your life may need an invitation to share their hearts with you. Again, relationships work best when both parties are able to open up and feel heard.

### The I-Have-to-Talk-about-Everything Soul

In my teen years, I had a crush on a boy, and he liked me, too. We went out with a group of friends, and as we were getting out of the car to walk into a restaurant, I stumbled. He said, "Hurry up," and I thought I heard a slight edge to his voice, a note of annoyance. His tone hurt my feelings. It bothered me all through our meal, nibbling at the back of my mind, and finally, after the meal, I couldn't stand it any longer. I pulled him aside and told him I thought he'd been impatient with me and that I felt hurt. He hardly remembered the interaction, much less what tone of voice he had used. To his credit, he tried to make an "I'm sorry" face, but I could see "You're needy and weird" written all over it instead. I ended up feeling worse instead of better, and our interactions became increasingly stiff for the rest of the afternoon.

I learned a lesson that day: people need grace. Sure, we need to talk about issues, but we also need to install an Oversensitivity Gauge inside that helps us to evaluate which issues are worth bringing up and which should fall under the "love covers over a multitude of sins" umbrella (1 Peter 4:8).

Big feelers tend to feel in extremes: *If I don't talk about every hurt feeling or slight disagreement, this relationship is dishonest.* But I urge you to cultivate wisdom in when to talk . . . and when to let things go. It's not that we shouldn't be honest or shouldn't bring up things that are bothering us, but we have to learn to let some things slide.

### The Too-Fast-Too-Soon Soul

I still remember the first time I hung out with my soon-to-be-best-friend, Sara. She had been at my house for a whopping thirty minutes—maybe less. Laughter was flowing, the list of things we shared in common was growing, and as I stood at the end of my bed, folding a washcloth (why I was folding laundry while a friend was over, I couldn't tell you), an epiphany rang inside: *This girl is the best friend I've ever had.* I know. Kinda dramatic after only thirty minutes, right? My instinct ended up proving right—almost thirty years later, we are still cross-country besties—but thankfully, I had the wisdom not to inflict my too-fast-too-soon affection on poor, unsuspecting Sara for a while.

Bless us, when we sense a kindred spirit, our hearts practically leap from our chests in the thrill of discovery and connection. But even though this love is ultimately a reflection of God's heart, we benefit from some practical wisdom. It's wise to get to know people bit by bit, rather than purchasing BFF necklaces on the first day we meet. It's also wise not to announce our feelings too quickly, lest we overwhelm (also known as "freak out and drive away") the object of our newfound affection.

"Be as shrewd as snakes and as innocent as doves," Jesus told his disciples (Matthew 10:16). In context, he was talking about dealing with non-Christians while doing the work of the Lord, but the advice has application in many relationships. We can preserve the innocent, childlike part of our hearts that meets new people and immediately sings, "Best friends forever," but we can also be shrewd enough—wise enough—to withhold offers of blood pacts while we are still in the getting-to-know-you stage. Not only does this allow us to get to know people more fully (because first impressions can be incomplete and inaccurate), it also allows new people to warm to us in their own time, without emotional pressure.

## The I-Need-to-Take-God's-Place Soul

As we discussed in chapter 8, sometimes the intensity of our love makes us try to be God for people. To heal all their wounds. Fix all their problems. Share all their joys to the full. Be ever-present for their highs and their lows.

As devoted and faithful as we want to be, we all have limits. Time limits, resource limits, emotional limits. We can't be another person's everything—we are doomed to fail them, not to mention exhaust ourselves. Only God can be their everything—it turns out he is quite good at his job—and as much as we love people and long to support them, we are called to point people to God as the source of unfailing love and unflagging devotion.

## A RESURRECTING LOVE

We began this chapter with Ruth and Naomi: a broken old woman, a devoted young woman, deep feelers both, starting a new stage of life together. The Bible doesn't depict all the details of their new life, but it tells us that sometime after Naomi disavowed her old name—after she distanced herself from her old life, her old self—declaring herself permanently lost, forever bitter, forever Mara, a surprising change happened: Naomi woke up. She realized she'd been sitting at home, stuck in a cycle of mourning, but all that time she hadn't been mourning alone. She had Ruth, a young woman so devoted that the other townswomen said, "She is worth more than seven sons" (Ruth 4:15).

Naomi shook the cobwebs from her heart and started mothering again. She decided to find Ruth a husband to care for her. She taught Ruth how to pursue remarriage and navigate the complex courting rituals of Jewish culture. Ruth's love helped resurrect Naomi's heart, and in turn, Naomi resurrected Ruth's hopes of having a husband and family.

It's interesting to note that nowhere in the book of Ruth does Naomi verbally echo Ruth's eloquent declaration of devotion; we don't read any lines where Naomi says, "Oh, dear daughter, how could I live without you? You have restored life to my dying heart." No, Naomi reciprocated by *doing*. By serving. Even among deep feelers, we express our emotions in different ways. Some people's intense emotions get tangled inside, trapped, and they can't communicate all they feel, all they long to say. I wonder if Ruth received Naomi's advice and service as the loving act of devotion Naomi intended—I suspect she did.

This gives us one last helpful hint into finding peace and joy in our relationships. Don't expect others to know how to reciprocate the effusive love you give in the same manner you offer it. In a lifetime you may encounter a handful of sensitive souls who are like minded, able to express love for you in the same way you express it for them. Those relationships are precious jewels, but they are rare. The sooner you make peace with that, the less disappointed you will be in the rest of man- and womankind (not to mention your significant other, who is probably not wired with the same sensitivities you are). I'm not suggesting you become cynical—just realistic in your expectations. "It takes one to know one," as they say. And sometimes "it takes one to know how to love one."

The book of Ruth ends with Naomi grinning over a newborn grandbaby, Ruth's son. The whole town rejoiced with her: "Naomi," they said, "has a son" (Ruth 4:17). (Notice they didn't call her "Mara"—once more she was Naomi; once more she was sweet.)

Naomi came back from the brink of despair. Back to life, to hope, to laughter. And what helped her find the way? The love of a young woman with a wide-open heart and a gift for loyalty. The love of a deep feeler named Ruth.

Such is the power of relationships. Friendships may be messy at times and imperfect always, but they make life's madness worth bearing. Friendships are worth having, my friend.

## FEELING YOUR WAY FORWARD

### Prayer Prompt

> The LORD is a friend to those who fear him.
>> He teaches them his covenant.
> My eyes are always on the LORD,
>> for he rescues me from the traps of my enemies.
> Turn to me and have mercy,
>> for I am alone and in deep distress.
> My problems go from bad to worse.
>> Oh, save me from them all!
>
> PSALM 25:14-17, NLT

### Journal Prompts

1. Which relationship struggle do you most relate to: feeling insecure, being angry, dealing with old wounds, being easily offended, making things too much about you, or wanting to talk about every feeling? How might you begin to work on that?

2. How might you begin sharing more of your feelings—the good and the bad—with God?

3. What is going great in your relationships? What do you wish were different?

# CHAPTER 15

# INPUT OVERLOAD

Can we pause to address the elephant in the room—er, book? Previous generations of sensitive souls only had to manage the burdens of their families, friends, and local communities; you and I have to process all the pain and poverty and imperfection of the entire globe as it pours in through our devices. Our constantly connected world delivers a relentless flood of emotional input. It's no wonder our poor beleaguered membranes become overwhelmed. Sometimes they shut down and shut it all out, leaving us feeling distant and detached. Other times they break down and let it all flow in, leaving our emotions in a state of crisis.

For me, the emotional minefield of the news and social media is summed up in the story of the oak-tree man. I don't know his name, but I remember his story from the nightly news: how one wind-whipped, rain-slung Atlanta night, he loaded his family, a wife and two daughters, into their car on the side of the street.

Maybe it was a we-have-cabin-fever-so-let's-brave-the-rain-and-splurge-on-Chick-fil-A night, or maybe it was a Grandma's-sick-so-let's-cheer-her-up trip.

At any rate, at first the oak branches overhead provided shelter from the rain as the family struggled with umbrellas and car seats—but then came a violent ripping sound. In the wet dark, they couldn't see the ground heaving, the roots tearing loose from sodden soil, the ancient trunk leaning, falling, crashing down. The wife and both children were killed; the man survived. Their tragedy was just a passing mention on the evening news, barely forty-five seconds of airtime, but twenty years later, I carry that family with me. I still ache for that man, still pray for him, still carry a bit of his burden. Perhaps you have stories like this you carry too.

If you are a big feeler, you are going to be more deeply affected by suffering around the world. Once you invite the nightly 6:00 horrors into your home—*factions! flood! famine!*—they will want to unpack their suitcases and stay a night or two or ten. We have to be intentional about how often and to what extent we invite the burdens of acquaintances and strangers into our hearts—and onto our devices.

Although social media can be a source of connection, camaraderie, and creativity, dangers abound for the sensitive soul. Because once you see that picture with the poignant caption—*My neighbor's niece's cousin's toddler—see the adorable curls and ginormous angelic eyes?—is sick. Please pray and donate and join our weekly prayer chain*—you won't be able to un-see it. You won't be able to un-care. Of course, seeing and caring aren't bad things—they are reflections of God's heart! But as humans, we have limits—emotional and spiritual limits, time constraints, daily responsibilities—and so we must parcel out our energy and resources wisely. This allows us to concentrate wholeheartedly on seeing and caring about the people and problems God has assigned specifically to us.

## HOW MUCH MEDIA SHOULD YOU LET IN?

Let's talk about media habits that can help to preserve your seren-ity, not to mention your sanity. As overarching principles, keep in mind the biblical calls to fix our eyes on Jesus (see Hebrews 12:2) and to set our minds on things above rather than on earthly things (see Colossians 3:2). If we're not careful, the constant influx of media can consume our thoughts, our hearts, and our time. So what lifestyle choices can we make to cultivate the kind of thought life God wants us to have?

### 1. Know your limits and limit your exposure.

Different types of feelers have different relationships with social media, and we can all learn from one another. While the big feelers may find social media overwhelming, steady and reluctant feelers may not feel the same way. Because they are able to compart-mentalize emotions, steady and reluctant feelers can regulate how much others' struggles and heartaches affect them. That's a skill we big-feeling types would love to learn from you! However, I have some steady-feeling and reluctant-feeling friends who occasionally feel guilty about their strength—they see weepers like me getting undone by every sad post, and they wonder if their hearts are hard or unloving. While there may be times when you need the big-feeling types to soften you up, don't feel guilty for being wired the way you are—big feelers need you!

Only you know how much you can handle, but here are a few practices to try out.

- Keep a tight grip on your social media connections. You are not obligated to "friend" and "follow" the whole world.
- Take breaks from social media as needed. Most weekdays I post to my author accounts—and keeping up with readers is an absolute joy—but I no longer rely on social

media as a primary way of keeping up with family and personal friends. We keep up other ways.

- Limit how much news you watch . . . or go old school and switch to the newspaper instead. These days most of my news comes from reading the newspaper at Starbucks. I'm completely aware of the world's goings-on; I just prefer my news in print rather than pixels. I find the more clinical tone of newspapers a better fit for me emotionally. It also helps me to read words instead of viewing high-definition videos of anguished people wailing while maudlin soundtracks call to my tear ducts.
- It is okay—even godly—to empathize with and pray for hurting people. But remember that you don't have to commit the full force of your feelings to every problem or heartache you hear about.
- Beware the temptation to be drawn into others' conflicts when they use social media as a platform for venting.

And lest you think it's unrighteous to have some boundaries when it comes to your emotional intake—choosing *not* to engage in certain issues—take a look at this moment in Jesus' ministry:

> Someone in the crowd said to him, "Teacher, tell my brother to divide the inheritance with me."
> Jesus replied, "Man, who appointed me a judge or an arbiter between you?" Then he said to them, "Watch out! Be on your guard against all kinds of greed; life does not consist in an abundance of possessions."
> LUKE 12:13-15

Although I'm sure Jesus cared about this man and his problem, he refused to be drawn into a family spat. The Lord did go on to tell a story about greed and how we should focus less on estate planning and more on where-will-my-soul-go-when-I-die planning, but that was as far as he engaged. He kept moving with his life and ministry.

## 2. Recognize levels of intimacy and influence.

That leads us to a related topic: levels of intimacy. Our emotional energy—vast as it may feel—does have limits and needs to be rationed. If we use up all our emotional energy on the heartache of people we barely know—or never will know—we won't have much left for the people whose daily lives are intimately and inextricably intertwined with ours: significant others, children, parents, dearest friends.

Like it or not, we have tiers of relationships:

- an inner circle (family and close friends)
- a daily circle (local church family, coworkers, classmates)
- a shoulder-brushing fellowship circle (neighborhood and casual friends)
- a broad circle (acquaintances and local community members)
- the rest of the world (all humans, plus Labrador retrievers, whom I consider to be basically human)

If you think this concept of levels of relationship is unspiritual, think again! Even Jesus had different circles of human relationships:

- the three (see Matthew 17:1-9)
- the twelve apostles (see Luke 6:12-16)
- the group of followers who traveled with him (see Mark 15:40-41; Luke 8:1-3)
- his family (see Luke 8:19-21; John 19:25-27)

- the crowd that believed in him (see Matthew 4:23–5:2; Luke 14:25-27)
- the communities he traveled to and through (see Luke 8:1)
- the nation of Israel (see Matthew 10:5-6)
- the world (see Matthew 28:18-20)

Jesus devoted his attention to each group differently.* He frequently spent time alone with the Twelve, retreating (as best he was able) to secluded places so he could teach them privately. Close as he was to his disciples, he was closer still to three of the Twelve: James, John, and Simon Peter. Jesus reserved a few unique experiences for these men (see Matthew 17:1-8; 26:36-38). And like us, he had other, larger groups of people he dearly loved but with whom he spent less time.

I find it helpful to keep in mind that other people's emotions should affect me in accordance with the position they occupy in my heart. In other words, a heartache in my son's life is going to affect me more deeply and for a longer period of time than, say, a heartache befalling an acquaintance on Facebook or a stranger across the globe.

Of course, these soft hearts of ours may struggle to differentiate the intensity of our responses. We big feelers are often tempted to fling all the feels at all the people all the time. When an acquaintance or stranger's suffering enters our radar, we have to help our emotions react accordingly by reminding ourselves, *As awful as this tragedy is for that person I knew in middle school or that suffering stranger in Mongolia, I can't unleash the full force of my empathy here for a prolonged period of time.* It's not that we can't feel—or don't feel—for that person. Our thin membranes ensure that their pain is bound to cross into our hearts. But we try to temper the

---

* You may be surprised at how far down the list I put Jesus' family. As his ministry grew more controversial, Jesus' relationship with his biological family became more difficult and distant (see Mark 3:31-35). However, after his resurrection, we find Mary and his brothers praying with the early church (see Acts 1:14). Several of Jesus' brothers played key leadership roles in the early church.

intensity of the dosage of pain we receive and limit the length of our engagement.

If you are a steady feeler, you may not face this struggle as often, but you will occasionally encounter stories and sorrows that kick you in the gut and leave you winded. They may catch you off guard and unprepared because you're usually so steady! In those times, you also may need to limit the extent of your exposure and the length of your engagement.

Reluctant feelers, who prefer life to be orderly and logical, sometimes need the opposite advice: you may need to consciously choose emotional engagement with the outside world. Yes, our world is a messy place—so much drama and pain, so much sin and hurt—and you may prefer to focus on your own problems and stay out of other people's messes, but remember: the rest of us need you! Although you may be great at delineating emotional boundaries—"I'm not getting caught up in that—it's not my problem"—you don't want to harden yourself against *all* problems outside your immediate relationships. If you find yourself in a place where little moves you and everything feels distant, perhaps your heart is becoming too clinical and it's time to practice some intentional empathy.

So what do we do with someone else's burden once it comes inside? As we discussed in chapter 8, we wrap it up in a new membrane, or container—specifically prayer and compassion, and sometimes action—and as we pray, we propel that person's need, along with the emotions that accompany it, into God's capable hands. And there we leave it, knowing he is the one who can actually do something about it.

Sometimes the only thing we can do is pray, but other times our prayer reveals actions we can take—and when that happens, we should act! God gives us empathy not *just* as an emotion, but also as a catalyst for service. As feelers, we are not just God's heart here on earth; we are also his hands and feet. And when our hearts reveal acts of compassion and service that God is calling us to do, let us put our hands to work fulfilling our God-ordained role the best we can. What a relief that action can be! Instead of sitting around feeling helpless, we have an outlet—something to do with all our compassion. Our actions may not completely resolve the problem or alleviate the suffering, but at least they are a start, and we can rest easier knowing God can finish the work he has begun through us. And then—again—we circle back to prayer, where we place our burdens in God's almighty hands.

Yes, I know this is easier said than done—and certainly easier said than *felt*. But it's a necessary emotional skill. An essential skill we must continue to hone over time—for the rest of our time here on earth.

This earth of ours seems to grow larger *and* smaller every day, as technology transforms and intertwines our relationships—even from across the globe. As with most changes, the increased connection brings both blessings and difficulties. Although some of us may long for simpler days and wish we lived in the pre-smartphone, pre-twenty-four-hour-news-cycle world, God in his wisdom put us in this one. And it's up to us to adopt an intentional, healthy lifestyle that doesn't drive us to hermitude but allows us to be good neighbors and loving friends and family members. People who aren't afraid to open the windows and doors and let the fresh air—and friends—come inside.

## FEELING YOUR WAY FORWARD

### Prayer Prompt

> Your eternal word, O LORD,
> stands firm in heaven.
> Your faithfulness extends to every generation,
> as enduring as the earth you created.

Your regulations remain true to this day,
    for everything serves your plans.
If your instructions hadn't sustained me with joy,
    I would have died in my misery.
I will never forget your commandments,
    for by them you give me life.
I am yours; rescue me!
    For I have worked hard at obeying your
        commandments. . . .
Oh, how I love your instructions!
    I think about them all day long.

PSALM 119:89-94, 97, NLT

## Journal Prompts

1. What earthly things tend to take up a lot of your thoughts? How can you either think less about those things or bring God into your inner dialogue?

2. How does social media affect you? How would you describe its influence on your faith? Your relationships? Your spiritual and emotional health?

3. What one change would you like to make in your social media habits?

4. We talked about different categories of relationships in our lives (inner circle, daily circle, shoulder-brushing circle, etc.). Which person or group of people in your life would you like to devote more emotional energy to? How might you make room for that change?

# CHAPTER 16

# SHARING YOUR EMOTIONAL GIFTS WITH THE WORLD

It's 5 a.m., twenty-odd years ago. I'm a newlywed leading a campus ministry for my local church. Sleep, foul traitor, has abandoned me. My mind is a movie reel, splashing horror scenes across the backs of my eyelids.

First I flash back to yesterday's church staff meeting: "So apparently there is a conflict between several roommates in the campus ministry," my supervisor says. "They're about to tear each other to pieces. Someone on staff needs to help them work it out." As her eyes travel the room of full-time ministers and student interns, I try to fade into the couch pillows. *I am one with the paisley. I am one with the paisley. I am one with the—*

"Elizabeth! You're good at connecting with people and drawing out their feelings. This is the perfect job for you."

*Dang it.*

As she starts rattling off ideas—Scriptures to reference, questions to ask, solutions to suggest—my stomach coils into a knot.

My trembling fingers scribble notes. I make the calls, set up the appointment. By the time my husband and I have driven home—a twenty-minute crawl through the ever-present tangle of Atlanta traffic—I'm sure I have the beginnings of an ulcer. Possibly four, one for each girl I'm supposed to counsel.

Then my imagination flashes forward to the talk itself, set for five eternal days from now. I picture everything I should say, everything they might say, all the thousand ways this conversation could go sideways: Being driven out of the apartment by shouting girls. Being chased by parents with pitchforks. Facing an Inquisition-style trial. Being fired in public disgrace in front of the whole church.

For the five days preceding the talk, I can hardly eat. When my husband tries to talk to me, I am absent, dazed. I go through life robotically, counting the hours till my Death by Conflict Resolution.

I survive the talk—of course I survive. The girls hug it out and all is well: they love each other, they love me, the parents are happy, my supervisor is happy. No one but my husband knows what a heavy price I paid (and *he* paid) for that talk. I lost a week of my life just preparing for it, and I'm still twitchy for days afterward.

\*   \*   \*

It's 5 a.m. again, fifteen years later. An idea whispers me awake. The idea must find words, the words must be written, and the words must be written *now*. I spring out of bed in the dark, tiptoe past our babies' rooms—if they wake, all is lost—and sit at my computer, fingers typing as fast as they can but still not fast enough to keep up with the scenes playing out in my head. In one frenzied predawn hour, I bang out an entire script, a worship concept I've never seen before, blending acting with Scripture reading and congregational singing and musical performance—and in the deepest part of my soul, I know it: *This is from the Holy Spirit. A gift to my church. And it's going to help people.*

A few weeks later, on Easter morning, we perform the script (though *perform* isn't really the right word—as a congregation, we *participate*). People tell me it's the most emotional worship service we've had in years—maybe ever. The script goes on to be used in multiple churches for thousands of people. Every time I watch, I sit in wonder. It came from the Holy Spirit, and I got to be the pen that wrote it down.

*     *     *

Two sleepless early mornings, two opportunities to serve my local church, two dramatically different responses on my part. Technically I was "successful" in both situations, but while one brought out my emotional best, the other brought out my worst.

Determining how best to use your gifts at home, at work, and in God's church can be tricky business for anyone. And I would contend that such decisions can be even more complex for us sensitive souls.

## WHERE DO I GO FROM HERE?

Let's take a moment to consider your next steps. You've identified your strengths, become more aware of potential pitfalls, collected a cache of helpful Scriptures, and cultivated some strategies for thriving with your emotional makeup. We've spent a lot of time looking inward, but now it's time to look outward. How might God want you to use the gifts he has entrusted to you? What might he have in mind for your life moving forward? With your unique wiring, how can you best contribute to your family, your community, your church, your vocation, and the Kingdom of God?

I picture God handing out gifts to newborns: "Oh, how this one will sing! And how this one will encourage. This one's a teacher!

And what a servant this one will be." How excited he must have been to give us our one-of-a-kind strengths and passions. What fun he must have had envisioning us putting his gifts to work for his people and his glory!

> In his grace, God has given us different gifts for doing certain things well. So if God has given you the ability to prophesy, speak out with as much faith as God has given you. If your gift is serving others, serve them well. If you are a teacher, teach well. If your gift is to encourage others, be encouraging. If it is giving, give generously. If God has given you leadership ability, take the responsibility seriously. And if you have a gift for showing kindness to others, do it gladly.
>
> ROMANS 12:6-8, NLT

Think about your gifts—especially your emotional gifts, which we've taken so much time exploring in these pages. You don't have to hold an official title or position in order to use those talents to their full capacity. As we've seen, you can serve people as quietly and unofficially as you like. (See chapter 2 to remind yourself of all the ways you can use your emotions to bless others!)

We have only twenty-four hours in a day, and only eighty or ninety years or so (Lord willing) in which to use our gifts. We all have to make choices about which jobs, roles, and responsibilities to accept and which to forgo. If you need help making some of those choices, this chapter is for you. While no book or person can answer the questions only you can answer, the following prompts and guiding principles may help you choose paths that bring out your best.

### What are you uniquely suited to do?

You've probably figured out that your gifts make you perfectly suited for some roles and responsibilities but mismatched in others.

Let's start with big feelers. Many of us are drawn to occupations and volunteer positions where we help others; our empathy and ability to walk in other people's shoes make us uniquely suited for such roles. Social work, teaching, medicine, ministry, service—these are positions that can put our compassion and insight to excellent use. But the very aspects of these roles that call to our compassion can also burden it, and they can take a heavy emotional toll. Sometimes our hearts pull us toward a position we think will fulfill us, but we soon find ourselves overwhelmed, unable to detach from its emotional weight.

We can (and should) grow and stretch ourselves, but research has shown that some aspects of our basic personality and temperament are hardwired into us:

> Bill Gates is never going to be Bill Clinton, no matter how he polishes his social skills, and Bill Clinton can never be Bill Gates, no matter how much time he spends alone with a computer.
>
> We might call this the "rubber band theory" of personality. We are like rubber bands at rest. We are elastic and can stretch ourselves, but only so much.[17]

The question is: Which roles are worth the pain of stretching our emotional limits, and how far can we stretch without breaking? Only you can decide that. But keep in mind that every job, responsibility, and role carries inherent emotional stress that sometimes strains our sensitivities. Even independent pursuits and positions carry some emotional pressure. Although my career as a writer is in some ways a solitary endeavor, I still have deadlines dangling overhead, editors and marketing people to work with, readers to interact with, and speeches to give.

We all have to learn how to manage stress: dealing with conflict, meeting deadlines, disappointing others, and being disappointed by others. We sensitive souls have to learn how to handle stress in every area of life, and some of us may have to work harder than others at doing so. Our goal should not be to avoid all stress (an impossible goal); rather, our aim should be to identify roles with the kinds of stress (and levels of stress) that we can manage successfully. At the same time, we should strive to grow in how we manage conflict and difficulty.

Steady feelers, because you are blessed with high emotional intelligence and a steady personality, you can thrive in a variety of settings, and you will especially shine in roles where you influence others and bring people together. You may be a quiet leader, helping others to understand one another and forge connections, or you may step out front, building unity and pointing the way forward. In the working world, your emotional balance makes you an ideal candidate for positions that call for wisdom. When it comes to service, you may be a gifted mentor, a community organizer, or an inspiring fundraiser. In whatever role you take on, your compassionate side grants you insights into others' needs, and your logical side helps to keep your boundaries in place so you don't often get overwhelmed.

But don't take your boundaries for granted. As strong and resilient as you are, you still need replenishing—and occasionally protecting. Keep a gauge on your heart, and watch for warning signs of being overwhelmed: Are you feeling drained? Uninspired? Are you losing your enthusiasm for roles and responsibilities you usually enjoy? All these may be signs that you have spent too much emotional energy and need refilling. In those moments, take the time you need to let God and others fill you up again.

Reluctant feelers, your gifts for reason and fairness make you a master at decision making and problem solving. You shine in roles where you need to collect information, evaluate choices, weigh pros and cons, assemble teams, and make difficult choices. You may be adept at handling plans, regulations, statistics, information, or laws. Chances are, you keep details organized and organizations detailed! Whatever your role, the people around you probably depend on you to keep things amicable. When tempers rise and feelings cloud judgment, you serve as the fair-minded peacekeeper who speaks truth—and calms storms.

Occasionally, you may find yourself baffled—or even frustrated—by others' high-flying feelings. In those situations, it's wise to invite a steady feeler or big feeler to help you translate. In those moments of partnership, your strengths can complement each other in a beautiful example of the body of Christ working in harmony, each part doing its work:

> There are different kinds of spiritual gifts, but the same Spirit is the source of them all. There are different kinds of service, but we serve the same Lord. God works in different ways, but it is the same God who does the work in all of us.
>
> 1 CORINTHIANS 12:4-6, NLT

## Is this position right for you?

So how do you decide if a new role or responsibility is a good fit? Here are a few questions to ask yourself when assessing a current role or considering a new one:

- Does this role or position bring out the best in me? Why or why not?
- Do I like the person I am when I fill this role?
- Am I the Christian I want to be when I hold this role? Am I the friend/roommate/student/spouse/parent/caretaker I want to be? Why or why not?

- Is the stress inherent in this role something I can learn to manage by disciplining my thought patterns and implementing healthy boundaries (emotional boundaries, time boundaries, etc.)?
- Are the rewards of this position (and remember, rewards come in many forms—relational, emotional, occupational, financial, and so on) worth the emotional cost?

Only you can assess whether or not a role is right for you. However, it can be illuminating to also ask people who know you well, "Do you think such-and-such a role is a good fit for me? Why or why not?"

As you move through life with your emotional nature—be it steady, logical, or sensitive—I pray you find the places and people God wants you to touch.

> To each one of us grace has been given as Christ apportioned it. . . . So Christ himself gave the apostles, the prophets, the evangelists, the pastors and teachers, to equip his people for works of service, so that the body of Christ may be built up until we all reach unity in the faith and in the knowledge of the Son of God and become mature, attaining to the whole measure of the fullness of Christ. . . .
>
> From him the whole body, joined and held together by every supporting ligament, grows and builds itself up in love, as each part does its work.
>
> EPHESIANS 4:7, 11-13, 16

You have work to do for God—people to love and places to serve. And your emotions can be priceless assets to help you fulfill those callings. As you offer your distinct wiring and talents to

God for his purpose and glory, I pray you feel his joy. Even now he is cheering you on, eager to say, "Well done, good and faithful servant. Come share my happiness" (see Matthew 25:21).

## FEELING YOUR WAY FORWARD

### Prayer Prompt

> Let the morning bring me word of your unfailing love,
> for I have put my trust in you.
> Show me the way I should go,
> for to you I entrust my life.
> Rescue me from my enemies, LORD,
> for I hide myself in you.
> Teach me to do your will,
> for you are my God;
> may your good Spirit
> lead me on level ground.

PSALM 143:8-10

### Journal Prompts

1. Describe a time when you felt most fulfilled. What role were you playing? Why did it bring you so much joy? How did it complement your feeling type?

2. Take a moment to dream: If you could do anything with your life, what would it be? Don't just think "career"; think also about roles you'd like to play at home or in your church, and consider ways you'd like to contribute to your family or community. Why does that role appeal to you?

3. If you are evaluating a new role or responsibility, journal your responses to the questions on pages 253–254.

# CHAPTER 17

# HOW GOD FEELS ABOUT FEELERS

We have covered a lot of ground in this book. We've explored our strengths, examined our weaknesses, and equipped ourselves with Scriptures to help us grow. We've encountered some of the specific emotions that can trip us up: sadness, anxiety, cynicism, guilt. I pray you have already begun stepping out into the world more boldly: more confident in the person God made you to be, more aware of all the ways he longs to use you, more at home in your own skin—even if that skin is thinner (or thicker!) than you'd like it to be. As we finish our journey through these pages, I want to remind you who you are before God—how much he loves you, how sensitive *he* is in his dealings with you.

Whenever I'm visited by unwanted doubts about the way I'm wired—*Are you sure you like me, God? Are you sure all these big feelings of mine aren't annoying or overwhelming to you?*—I find it helpful to go back to Scripture. You and I are not the first feelers God has ever dealt with—far from it! Let's take a stroll through the Scriptures to see how God treats people with various emotional types. We'll drop in on some highlights—actually more like lowlights—in some of our Bible heroes' lives to see how God responds to them . . . and to us.

## BIG FEELER HANNAH

Oh, Hannah. This woman has my heart. Perhaps you remember her story, told in 1 Samuel 1–2. Adored by her husband but unable to conceive; mocked and humiliated by Peninnah, a rival wife who had babies to spare. I suspect Hannah was a big feeler, because at one point she was so upset by Peninnah's cruelty that she refused to eat. And just take a look at her passionate prayer life:

> Once when they had finished eating and drinking in Shiloh, Hannah stood up. Now Eli the priest was sitting on his chair by the doorpost of the Lord's house. In her deep anguish Hannah prayed to the Lord, weeping bitterly. And she made a vow, saying, "Lord Almighty, if you will only look on your servant's misery and remember me, and not forget your servant but give her a son, then I will give him to the Lord for all the days of his life, and no razor will ever be used on his head."
>
> As she kept on praying to the Lord, Eli observed her mouth. Hannah was praying in her heart, and her lips were moving but her voice was not heard. Eli thought she was drunk and said to her, "How long are you going to stay drunk? Put away your wine."
>
> "Not so, my lord," Hannah replied, "I am a woman who is deeply troubled. I have not been drinking wine or beer; I was pouring out my soul to the Lord. Do not take

your servant for a wicked woman; I have been praying
here out of my great anguish and grief."

1 SAMUEL 1:9-16

Notice the emotional language here: "deep anguish," "weeping
bitterly," "great anguish and grief." Hannah was weeping, lost in
tears and prayer. Her prayers were so intense she was undone—
looked drunk, even!—and nearly got herself kicked out of the
Tabernacle. Hannah's passion captures the attention of Eli the
priest—and of God:

Eli answered, "Go in peace, and may the God of Israel
grant you what you have asked of him." . . .
　　Early the next morning they arose and worshiped
before the LORD and then went back to their home
at Ramah. Elkanah made love to his wife Hannah,
and the LORD remembered her. So in the course of
time Hannah became pregnant and gave birth to a
son. She named him Samuel, saying, "Because I asked
the LORD for him."

1 SAMUEL 1:17, 19-20

*The Lord remembered her.*
Surely these are four of the most poignant words in the Bible.
The Lord remembered her tears, her prayers, her hurt. He
remembered her promise to him—and Eli's to her. And he gave
her a son—a son whom she gave back to God, a boy who heard
the voice of God, a prophet who grew up to lead a nation.
What a story.
What a God.

## STEADY FEELER PAUL

In the apostle Paul we find a complex personality, a fascinating example of the steady feeler. His intensity and passion made him a powerful teacher and effective evangelist; his logic and rhetoric made him a persuasive writer; his steady conviction made him a competent church builder. His courage and constancy were rounded out by great compassion. But as caring as he was, his decision making was not compromised by conflict, others' opinions, or his own personal needs.

In Acts 16, we find a classic example of Paul's passion and practicality working hand in hand. While preaching in the city of Philippi, Paul and his companion, Silas, were arrested on false charges, beaten, and jailed. How did they respond to the injustice and humiliation? What did they do when they couldn't sleep due to their wounds? They pushed past the pain and fear to praise God in prayer and song, loud enough for all the other prisoners to hear:

> About midnight Paul and Silas were praying and singing hymns to God, and the other prisoners were listening to them. Suddenly there was such a violent earthquake that the foundations of the prison were shaken. At once all the prison doors flew open, and everyone's chains came loose. The jailer woke up, and when he saw the prison doors open, he drew his sword and was about to kill himself because he thought the prisoners had escaped. But Paul shouted, "Don't harm yourself! We are all here!"
>
> ACTS 16:25-28

Paul's suffering did not bring out hidden stores of bitterness— *Why would God allow this? We were serving him, and this is the reward we get?*—but rather a heart filled with gratitude, humility, and love.

Feelings that overflowed into song and preached a poignant sermon all their own.

Paul and Silas's heartfelt response inspired in turn a remarkable response from God: an earthquake so strong it set free not only Paul and Silas but every other prisoner in the jail! And in the tumultuous aftermath, Paul's steadiness shone. Realizing the jailer was about to commit suicide, Paul thought fast and acted graciously to save this man—his enemy. And he didn't just save the jailer's life physically; Paul also helped to save him spiritually. Paul set aside the pain of his wounds, the humiliation of his arrest, and the shock of an earthquake to share the gospel with the very man responsible for his suffering. That night, the jailer and his entire family turned to the Lord and were baptized (verses 31-34). A story that began in hatred and blood ended in salvation and joy, thanks to God's power at work—shaking the earth and shaking up hearts—and the faithful efforts of his unshakable servant Paul.

## RELUCTANT FEELER ABRAHAM

Abraham's nephew Lot was in danger, his city's doom a foregone conclusion. The Lord was sending his angels to the city of Sodom—Lot's home—and they carried destruction with them. How did reluctant feeler Abraham respond? Did he throw himself at the angels' feet, weeping and pleading for mercy for his nephew? Did he offer up eloquent, emotional prayers? No. Abraham kept his cool and began a humble, reverent (and convincing!) negotiation:

> "Will you sweep away the righteous with the
> wicked? What if there are fifty righteous people in
> the city? Will you really sweep it away and not spare the
> place for the sake of the fifty righteous people in it? Far
> be it from you to do such a thing—to kill the righteous
> with the wicked, treating the righteous and the wicked

alike. Far be it from you! Will not the Judge of all the earth do right?"

The LORD said, "If I find fifty righteous people in the city of Sodom, I will spare the whole place for their sake."

Then Abraham spoke up again: "Now that I have been so bold as to speak to the Lord, though I am nothing but dust and ashes, what if the number of the righteous is five less than fifty? Will you destroy the whole city for lack of five people?"

"If I find forty-five there," he said, "I will not destroy it."

GENESIS 18:23-28

Every time I read this story, I shake my head in wonder. I half expect lightning to crackle from the pages as an enraged God shows Abraham who's boss: "How dare you question my ways, you insolent worm? I am the great I Am! I make the rules!" But no, our compassionate, fair-minded God listens! More, he *adjusts his plans*—simply because Abraham had the courage to ask—and ask wisely.

Abraham kept talking, God kept listening, and eventually Abraham "talked God down" to ten people: "For the sake of ten, I will not destroy it," God promised (Genesis 18:32). Of course, we all know Sodom and its sister city, Gomorrah, were destroyed anyway, because God could not find even ten righteous souls within Sodom's walls.

But even though the cities fell, God was not done showing kindness. For Abraham's sake, God sent angels to rescue Lot and his family (see Genesis 19). What a comfort to realize that God listens to us. Welcomes our respectful questions and thoughts. Cares for our families. And sometimes—oh, wonder of wonders—he changes his plans.

* * *

When we take all these stories together—stories of real people with different emotional makeups, people in raw moments of crisis, heartache, and despair—we find a God who is patient, empathetic, kind. A Father who is willing to hear and eager to help.

You'll notice that God didn't erase these people's problems—Hannah still shared her husband with a rival wife; Paul still faced persecution; Abraham still witnessed the destruction of his nephew's home—but God comforted and strengthened and helped them through their difficulties.

Of course God expects us to repent when we sin, and he wants us to grow in the way we handle adversity. But he loves us even so. Even while. Even though. And God's desire for us to grow—even urging us to move toward growth—in no way diminishes his love for us. His *like* of us. His belief in who we can be.

As you finish this book, you may have a number of burdens still weighing on your heart. As much as you are striving to grow, that growth may be happening more slowly than you'd like. I pray you will have eyes to see God's love and special care for you. His willingness to connect with you where you are today, so he can help you mature into the place you want to be tomorrow.

Let these biblical examples remind us: sometimes when we seek help or relief from God, we look for the wrong things as proof of God's care. We look for escape, release from pain, freedom from difficulty—and in our tunnel vision, we miss God's other gifts, his sustaining kindnesses. Even if your life feels crushing, disappointing—even when the sorrows of this life feel beyond bearing—God still hears you and helps you. Even when you can't see or feel him.

If you, like Hannah and Paul and Abraham, have been suffering but not seeing relief, not getting the answers to prayer you wish God would give . . . is he giving you other things? Maybe even *better* things? Is he giving wisdom to counsel you? Friends to support you? Joy to sustain you?

Even when life beats us up—and we beat ourselves up—God is there. And if we'll learn to look for his loving hand, we will find it.

## IT TAKES ONE TO LOVE ONE

God loves feelers, my friends. God himself is a feeler. And he knows how to love feelers of all kinds. He shoulders our sadness, counts every tear:

> You keep track of all my sorrows.
> > You have collected all my tears in your bottle.
> > You have recorded each one in your book.
> PSALM 56:8, NLT

But it wasn't enough for God to merely shoulder and count. He sent his own Son to live among us—more, *as one of us*—so that he would understand all we suffer, all we feel:

> Since we have a great High Priest who has entered heaven, Jesus the Son of God, let us hold firmly to what we believe. This High Priest of ours understands our weaknesses, for he faced all of the same testings we do, yet he did not sin. So let us come boldly to the throne of our gracious God. There we will receive his mercy, and we will find grace to help us when we need it most.
> HEBREWS 4:14-16, NLT

Do you understand what this means for us? Jesus came to earth and experienced all the feels just like we do. The only difference (this teeny-tiny thing)? He never sinned (and of course it's not teeny-tiny at all). But God sent him here so he could better understand us—and so we could *know* he understands. So he could say, "I've felt that too. I've been tired like that. Lonely like that. Hurt like that."

And it's not just the big feelers he relates to; Jesus, the complete human, the man who walked this earth with his emotions always in perfect balance, understands us all. Like a steady feeler, he felt intensely yet maintained the courage and determination to keep moving forward, to always do the right thing. Like a reluctant feeler, Jesus was unprejudiced by his affection for people, unaffected by public opinion: he honored truth—and God—above all.

In this Jesus is like his Father—the Father who breathed life and breath into us all, designed our inmost being, and understands who we are, how we think, all we feel. The Father of the reluctant feeler, the steady feeler, the big feeler, and every shade of feeler in between.

Our God is compassionate. He loves who we are and how he made us. He loves watching us (and helping us) feel and love and grow:

> The LORD your God is living among you.
>     He is a mighty savior.
> He will take delight in you with gladness.
>     With his love, he will calm all your fears.
>     He will rejoice over you with joyful songs.
>
> ZEPHANIAH 3:17, NLT

Do you hear the love in these words? Can't you feel it—the understanding that covers all sin, the longing that bursts into song, the yearning that draws you in close?

He delights in you, his darling child.

You make him sing.

You.

Yes, you.

You, with all the feelings.

## THE BEST THING EVER

It's morning, barely. A hint of gray leaks through cracks in the blinds, nudging my exhausted eyelids. I nudge back, squeezing my eyes more tightly shut.

But my alarm clock is already at the door. The doorknob gives a clumsy rattle—left-right-left-left-right-left, silence. A little grunt of frustration. Eyes still shut, I can't help but smile. The would-be intruder tries again: left-right-left-right-right-right, *click*.

I hear a whoosh of air as the door swings open, then the soft shuffle-tap of happy feet on the wood floor beside my bed. A *swish* and tug, a feeling of almost falling, as dimpled fists grip the comforter and start to pull it off my body, toward the floor, in an attempt to climb up. Without opening my eyes, I reach a hand down, hook it under the arms I know are upstretched and waiting, and pull my daughter into bed beside me.

With a small sigh she slithers under the comforter, nestling her warm body against mine. A perfect fit. Quiet we lie, mother-daughter puzzle pieces. Her soft curls tickle my cheeks, her warm cheeks nuzzle my neck. I smile, drifting back into half-dreams. After a while, a pudgy hand pats my face. Warm breath brushes my ear. A little voice whispers, "Mommy, you and me are the best thing ever." Every sleeping thing in me lifts and sings, wakes in wonder.

I manage words: "Yes, darling, we are." I open my eyes to the sun.

\* \* \*

I think about that morning—those sparkling, transcendent seconds of purest love—when I think about God the Father. How he feels about us. How we his children can feel about him.

*God, you and me are the best thing ever.*

Because the thing is, he feels the same way. He felt it first, said it first, proved it first: *You and me are the best thing ever.*

Talk about all the feels. All the home-at-last, known-at-last, safe-at-last feels.

You and God, the best thing ever.

Forever and ever.

# ACKNOWLEDGMENTS

People often picture writing as a solitary, angsty endeavor—and sure, the drafting phase can be like that—but in truth, writing is a profound work shared by many. What a privilege it is to share the journey with family and friends, and then to work alongside others, each one offering their God-given talents, together making something that none of us could do alone.

People step in to share specific burdens and joys, but God is present for all of it: every scriptural "aha" moment, every step of personal transformation, every moment a word hits the page. The thrill as he whispers, guides, and inspires is beyond words: sacred, life changing, soul filling.

And then there are the amazing humans who share the journey. Over the years my husband, Kevin, has become an expert at being the spouse of a writer. During the writing of this book, he reached Jedi Master levels. He listens patiently, supports enthusiastically, knows I should never talk about feelings (especially feelings about whatever I'm writing) after 9 p.m., reminds me that books always come together by the grace of God, and—he should be sainted for this—on nights when I write late, he lets me come home to well-fed children and a gleaming kitchen. Thank you for sharing not just the writing life but *all* of life with me, and thank you for embracing all the feelings along the way.

Thank you to Cassidy, Blake, Avery, and Sawyer, for sharing me with this book for the past year. You don't make me feel guilty when I have to take time to write, and when we hang out as a family, you make me laugh till embarrassing things happen. Thank you for giving me all the happiest feelings.

My gracious in-laws, Bill and Glenda, cheerfully stepped in as piano-lesson chauffeurs, activity directors, and writing-night dinner providers. We couldn't have done our life without you this year, and we are forever thankful. Thank you for loving us the way you do; what a joy it is to share daily life together.

My family—Mom and Dad, David and Lisa, Jonathan and Talia, Alexandra and Jesse—has offered endless prayer support and encouragement not only for this book but for my entire (translation: twisty-turny and producing all the feels imaginable, including a few new emotions no one knew existed) writing journey. You are—and have always been—the place where it's safe to express and work through all the feelings. Thank you.

My writing partner, Emma, sacrificed numerous hours, even as she prepared for her own new job responsibilities, to help me craft this book. She knows what I want to say better than I do, and she lends me her words when I can't find my own. Best of all, she understands—and helps me process—all the feels all the time. Emma, your soul-sister friendship is one of my life's great gifts.

My agent, Jessie Kirkland, has gone far above the call of duty. Thank you for getting the idea from the get-go and for spending hours (so. many. hours.) brainstorming. Thank you for sharing your heart, insights, and friendship so generously.

This book wouldn't exist without the generosity of the Whitaker family, who allowed me to borrow their beautiful beach house (and sometimes their dog!) for some desperately needed writing retreats. I never could have finished this book without your kindness!

An eternal thank-you to our church family for making our life a joy. How we love serving God with you—you have our hearts.

To my fifth-grade writing students: Thank you for reminding me how much fun it is to sit down with a blank page and a pen (preferably one of Mrs. Thompson's Precious, Favorite, Multicolored Gel Pens) and write words that are all your own. Writing with you this year has been one of my all-time favorite things—and I mean that literally. (And you know I mean *literally* when I say "literally.")

The editorial team at Tyndale is a dream. Stephanie Rische, thank you for your gracious, intuitive edits. You understand the big feelings, and you handled mine with sensitivity and gentleness. Thank you for making the editing process a God-centered and— can this word even go with *editing*?—*encouraging* experience!

Jillian Schlossberg, fellow big feeler, thank you for understanding this book's message from the beginning. What a privilege and joy to work with a kindred spirit! Thank you for grasping the big picture; nurturing a fun, collaborative environment; and directing every step with passion. Sarah Atkinson, thank you for your guidance and enthusiasm and for providing the reluctant-feeler viewpoint to counterbalance all the big feels! Thank you for helping us envision ways this message could apply to all types of feelers. Brittany Bergman, thank you for devoting your eagle eye to this manuscript, catching all the mistakes that would have tormented my perfectionist soul had they escaped notice.

The design team at Tyndale is mind-blowingly talented, conveying deep spiritual messages through art. Libby Dykstra and Dean Renninger, all your insightful designs left me awed. Thank you for inviting me into the creative process and for pouring your skill—and heart—into making the cover such a delight.

A thousand thanks to Cassidy Gage, Colleen Gregorio, and the entire marketing team for your vision and dedication, helping this book find its place in the world. What a gift you are to me—and to every author blessed enough to have you in their cheering section.

Many thanks to the baristas at my Starbucks for putting extra love into my mochas. And thanks to the Tenors, George Winston, Taylor Swift, and Hans Zimmer ("The Marry Me Suite" from *Pirates of the Caribbean*—haunting and epic; I can't even) for creating the music I needed to write this book.

# NOTES

1. David D. Burns, *Feeling Good: The New Mood Therapy* (New York: Quill, 1999), xvii–xviii, 12.
2. Burns, xix.
3. Science shows that our thoughts about God not only affect our feelings and our mental and emotional health; they physically transform our brains. For a fascinating read on this, check out *The God-Shaped Brain: How Changing Your View of God Transforms Your Life* by Timothy R. Jennings.
4. And if you want more excellent strategies for categorizing and reframing distorted thoughts, or "cognitive distortions," Dr. Burns's book *Feeling Good* provides fantastic material that is easy to apply.
5. Elaine N. Aron, *The Highly Sensitive Person: How to Thrive When the World Overwhelms You* (New York: Harmony, 2016), xxi.
6. There are times when it's best *not* to bring up a feeling—at least not yet. For example, every time you feel insecure at work, it's probably not wise to run to your boss and ask if they're mad at you. At best you'll get a reputation as a delicate person they need to handle with kid gloves (which may be true, but still—this is the workplace). At worst you'll drive your boss nuts. Sometimes we need to give our feelings time to shake out and settle down before we speak up; other times we need to seek outside, objective input before we have a conversation.
7. This strategy is adapted from some methods offered by David D. Burns in his book *Feeling Good: The New Mood Therapy* (New York: Quill, 1999). See pages 53–55 and the vertical arrow technique on pages 263–71.
8. Timothy Keller, *Walking with God through Pain and Suffering* (New York: Penguin, 2013), 80.
9. I don't mean to offer trite answers to deep anguish—I recognize that some pain is unfathomable, some grief is insurmountable, and some wounds can't be healed this side of heaven. But this is not a book on suffering; it's a book

about feelings. And for now the best we can say is that there's a long view we humans can't see.

10. In writing this scene, I put Paul in an actual prison with cells and bars like one we might envision today. (He was jailed in such a prison with Silas in Acts 16, and he may have written 2 Timothy from the Mamertine dungeon.) However, some scholars think that Paul wrote the book of Philippians while he was under house arrest. (See https://www.biblica.com/resources/scholar-notes/niv-study-bible/intro-to-philippians/.)

11. See Isaiah 45:23; Deuteronomy 32:34-43; Isaiah 65:19; Revelation 21:4; Isaiah 35:5-7; 1 Thessalonians 4:13-18; Philippians 2:9-11; and Psalm 29:9.

12. C. S. Lewis, *Mere Christianity* (New York: HarperOne, 2001), 136–37.

13. *Blue Letter Bible*, "metanoia," accessed July 25, 2019, https://www.blueletterbible.org/lang/lexicon/lexicon.cfm?Strongs=G3341&t=NIV.

14. Paul J. Pastor, *The Face of the Deep* (Colorado Springs: David C. Cook, 2016), 36–37.

15. Robert E. Webber, *The Divine Embrace: Recovering the Passionate Spiritual Life* (Grand Rapids, MI: Baker Books, 2006), 20–21.

16. See 2 Samuel 1:17-27; Psalm 55:12-14; 2 Samuel 12:15-23; Psalm 55; Psalm 22:1-19; Psalm 6; Psalms 21, 23; Psalm 13; 25:16-18; Psalms 6, 69; 2 Samuel 12:15-23; Psalm 16:6; Psalm 51; 19:11-14; 25:7-11; Psalm 17:1-5; Psalms 14, 55; 2 Samuel 15:30-35; Psalm 69:1-4; Psalm 6:6; Psalm 21; Psalm 17:6-15; 86:14-17; 7:1-9.

17. Susan Cain, *Quiet: The Power of Introverts in a World That Can't Stop Talking* (New York: Broadway Books, 2013), 118.

# ABOUT THE AUTHOR

Elizabeth Laing Thompson writes at ElizabethLaingThompson.com about clinging to Christ through the chaos of daily life. As a minister, speaker, and novelist, she is always seeking humor in holiness and hope in heartache. She is the author of a novel for tweens and several Christian living books for women, including *When God Says, "Wait"* and *When God Says, "Go."* Elizabeth lives in North Carolina with her husband and children, and they were totally worth the wait.

Elizabeth's essays and poetry have appeared in many print and online publications, including Chicken Soup for the Soul, *Power for Living*, Proverbs 31 Ministries, *HuffPost*, *Mamalode*, *Coffee + Crumbs*, and *BonBon Break*.

After earning an English degree from Duke University, Elizabeth married her college sweetheart, Kevin Thompson, (after spending several years swooning over him from the passenger seat of his Dodge Avenger on the drive to church every Sunday). Together the newlyweds went to work serving campus ministries in North Carolina and Georgia. In 2013, after fourteen years devoted to student ministry, the Thompsons embarked on the adventure of a lifetime when they relocated to coastal North Carolina to plant a church.

Following a long struggle with infertility, Kevin and Elizabeth became the always exhausted but totally grateful parents of one large dog and four loud kids. More than twenty years into marriage, they still like each other even though Elizabeth regularly beats Kevin at Ping-Pong and buys too many overpriced mochas from Starbucks. Together they are raising an imperfect family and fighting to live and love God's way. They have frequent dance-party-related injuries and epic sock-toss battles. They call themselves the Crazies, because they really are—but most days, they mean that in a good way. They pray that the lessons they are learning will give others hope, encouragement, and many good laughs.

To connect with Elizabeth, visit her website, ElizabethLaingThompson.com. You can also find her on Facebook at facebook.com/aLizzyLife and on Instagram: @ElizabethLaingThompson.